THE BASICS

of

STARTING

a

CHILD-CARE BUSINESS

THE BUSINESS OF CHILD CARE

Marnie Forestieri

Gryphon House

LIBRARY OF CONGRESS CATALOGING-IN-PUBLICATION DATA

Library of Congress Control Number:2019955443

BULK PURCHASE

Gryphon House books are available for special premiums and sales promotions as well as for fund-raising use. Special editions or book excerpts also can be created to specifications. For details, call 800.638.0928.

DISCLAIMER

Gryphon House, Inc., cannot be held responsible for damage, mishap, or injury incurred during the use of or because of activities in this book. Appropriate and reasonable caution and adult supervision of children involved in activities and corresponding to the age and capability of each child involved are recommended at all times. Do not leave children unattended at any time. Observe safety and caution at all times.

This book is not intended to give legal or financial advice. All financial and legal opinions contained herein are from the personal research and experience of the author and are intended as educational material. Seek the advice of a qualified legal advisor or financial advisor before making legal or financial decisions.

⟦ CONTENTS ⟧

V
INTRODUCTION

1
CHAPTER 1:
OVERVIEW OF THE CHILD-CARE BUSINESS

17
CHAPTER 2:
BUSINESS-PLAN FUNDAMENTALS

29
CHAPTER 3:
CREATING YOUR MARKET ANALYSIS

45
CHAPTER 4:
PUTTING TOGETHER A FINANCIAL PLAN AND PROJECTIONS

67
CHAPTER 5:
YOUR ORGANIZATION, STRATEGY, AND IMPLEMENTATION

77
CHAPTER 6:
APPLYING FOR FINANCING AND MEETING WITH THE BANK

82
GLOSSARY

85
REFERENCES AND RECOMMENDED READING

93
INDEX

INTRODUCTION

The scene of a new parent dropping off her child for the first time is something professionals in the industry have been accustomed to for generations. Early childhood professionals have accepted the responsibility of helping young parents deal with sacrificing time with their children and missing important milestones such as their child's first smile or first words.

In the twentieth century, a time characterized by constant change, including a monumental campaign for women's rights, women were motivated to pursue a college education and join the workforce in greater numbers. Working parents today face the same challenges as the generations that preceded them on how to provide care for their young children while away at work. New parents are increasingly aware of current research that proves the importance of the first five years of a child's development, a period in which the brain develops faster than at any other time in a child's life. The unique characteristics of millennials and the generations born into the digital era will demand more from providers than just child-care services.

Young parents want educational offerings that will set up the foundation for their children's mental health, academic performance, and social skills. Therefore, the new generation of parents entering the market will redefine the necessary skills and credentials that it will take to join the ranks of early childhood professionals. Market demands will require programs to adapt, and programs that fail to do so might close due to financial pressures. The challenge—and the opportunity—is to be able to meet the new expectations of the next generation of parents.

DEVELOPING THIS SERIES

This book is the first in a series on starting and operating a child-care business. To provide information relevant to people who want to start their own child-care business and to directors who want to understand the business better, we sent out a needs-assessment survey to providers in our community serving different market segments. One of the survey findings is that, regardless of the organizational structure or business model, all child-care providers face the same challenges, such as operations, marketing, understanding finances, and customer service, on a daily basis.

In most cases, directors who responded to our survey say they report to an owner who handles the business side of the operation. One of the challenges of this dual-management system model—an investor/owner and a child-care director—is that it prevents directors from having a holistic view of the company. The high costs of setting up a program and lack of understanding of the business side of the industry, financing options, and challenges of opening a new business have kept educators on one side of the operations and owners on the other side. Owners handle the business side of the operation, including location selection, marketing the facility, securing financing, processing payroll, collecting money, and paying business expenses. Educators manage staff, provide customer service, and ensure the program's quality metrics. Nevertheless, directors know from experience that decisions made in one area of the company will affect the rest of the organization. Child-care directors who have an understanding of the business side of the operation will be able to operate more efficiently and will be able to respond faster to market trends as the organizations of the twenty-first century will demand internal departments to be interconnected.

This book is not intended to give legal or financial advice. All financial and legal opinions contained herein are from the personal research and experience of the author and are intended as educational material. Seek the advice of a qualified professional before making legal and financial decisions.

HOW TO USE THIS BOOK

This book is designed to explain how to start a child-care business, for those who wish to operate their own centers. But it can also be used by current and aspiring center directors to help them do their jobs better. You will find the following features throughout the book:

- **Main questions:** key questions that shape each chapter

- **Case studies:** real-life or fictional scenarios that illustrate key concepts

- **Build your knowledge:** exercises to help you apply the concepts you are learning

We will share case studies of providers in different settings, including home care, independent day care, franchised locations, as well as data provided by funding sources. Each chapter focuses on a specific area of business management, offering terminology and concepts to help you understand the ins and outs of the child-care business. At the end of each chapter, you will have the opportunity to build your knowledge with guided questions that will help you assess your progress.

BEFORE YOU BEGIN THE JOURNEY

Before you begin this journey, take stock of your strengths and don't forget to pack the following.

- **Your passion and the commitment to follow your heart:** What would you do with your time if you did not have to work for money? Your answer is a good clue to your passion. Combining your passion with your job leads to purpose. When I left the telecommunications industry, I was at the peak of my career. I had gained a reputation in that field, yet I was no longer passionate about the opportunities. I needed to find a new purpose, and in the field of child care I did. Purpose has nothing to do with income, status, or internal wiring—it is the fuel that starts your internal engine, enabling you to create change.

- **Your emotional intelligence:** In his *Harvard Business Review* article "What Makes a Leader?" Daniel Goleman explains that the most effective leaders have high levels of emotional intelligence. Self-awareness, self-regulation, motivation, empathy, and social skills enable leaders to maximize their own performance and that of their team. Empathy, in particular, is important. High-performing directors can relate to teachers because, in many cases, those directors started in the classroom themselves. They can build bridges with teachers and understand their daily struggles and challenges.

- **The right attitude:** James Strock states in his book *Serve to Lead: 21st-Century Leaders Manual* that leadership is about change. Similarly, Charles Darwin's theory of evolution reminds us that it is not the strongest nor the most intelligent species that survive; it is the ones that have the ability to respond to change.

- **Authenticity:** I have had many mentors with all sorts of personalities during my life. But these people all had one thing in common: They were true to who they were, and they encouraged me to follow that example. They made me realize that my uniqueness was a strength.

You don't need to have mastered all these qualities to begin your quest, but your path will be easier if you start with some skills in each of these areas. Growing into a high-performing director may be the hardest thing you have ever done, but take it from someone who has undergone the same process: It is worth every headache, frustrating moment, and sleepless night. Are you ready?

1
OVERVIEW OF THE CHILD-CARE BUSINESS

_GG_____

*Children are likely to live up to what
you believe of them.*

—LADY BIRD JOHNSON,
FORMER FIRST LADY OF THE UNITED STATES

MAIN QUESTIONS

» How and why did the child-care business develop?

» What are the market segments served by child-care businesses?

» What business models do child-care providers use
and how do those work?

» Which business model is right for you?

THE DEMAND

Child care represents a great opportunity for entrepreneurs because of the high demand for this service. Education researcher Suzanne Bouffard points out that 70 percent of single mothers and 80 percent of single fathers work outside the home. And in more than 60 percent of married households, both spouses work outside the home. According to their article for the Center for American Progress, "A New Vision for Child Care in the United States," Katie Hamm and Carmel Martin assert that about 12 million U.S. children younger than age five have working parents. For most of those families, child care is an economic necessity, as 65 percent of children under six years old have all their available parents in the labor force.

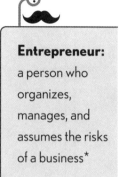

Entrepreneur: a person who organizes, manages, and assumes the risks of a business*

The early childhood industry in the United States emerged during the twentieth century in response to the expanding demand from employers and dual-income families for child-care services. As a result, a diverse patchwork of solutions has arisen to support the growing need. These solutions vary in cost, characteristics, level of quality, and organizational structure.

THE MARKET SEGMENTS

Policies, funding initiatives, tax credits, and regulations have shaped the child-care market. From a business perspective, we need to understand that financial statements and business plans will vary depending on the market segment and legal structure of an organization.

In a national landscape plagued by income inequality, different child-care solutions have developed organically to serve the different market segments. Sonia Michel, author of *Children's Interests/Mothers' Rights: The Shaping of America's Child Care Policy*, says that low-income parents typically enroll their children in publicly supported programs such as Head Start or programs that use Title I funding. Middle-class parents tend to choose group care centers, not-for-profit settings, or day-care solutions. Upper-class parents have a preference for in-home caregivers or child-care programs. Let's look at these segments more closely.

*Definitions are from *Merriam-Webster's Collegiate Dictionary*, 11th ed., or Investopedia.com

Programs Serving Low-Income Families

Providers serving low-income families are heavily dependent on public funding sources. Historically, as described in the *Handbook of Early Childhood Education*, edited by early childhood researcher Robert Pianta, a goal of public funding initiatives was to encourage low-income mothers to work to reduce their dependency on public assistance. These programs were intended to offer disadvantaged children a high-quality education so that they could eventually escape from poverty.

Head Start is a federal program that focuses on providing comprehensive services that promote school readiness, including education, health, and nutrition, for children from birth to age five.

Many Head Start programs also provide Early Head Start, serving infants, toddlers, and pregnant women and their families. According to the US Department of Health and Human Services Administration for Children and Families, during fiscal year 2010 Head Start received $7.2 billion to support about 900,000 children. Nevertheless, Head Start historically has not received funding sufficient to serve all the eligible families in the income bracket.

Fiscal year: an accounting period of twelve months; does not necessarily correspond to a calendar year

In response to growing demand, private providers have started businesses relying on other funding streams tied to specific goals at state and local levels. Providers serving low-income families vary tremendously in quality and size. Regrettably, that means that some children of low-income families participate in high-quality programs while others with a similar background can access only lower-quality child care. According to the Center for American Progress and the US Department of Education, most children who have access to preschool attend moderate-quality programs. However, African American children and children from low-income families are the most likely to attend low-quality preschool programs and, conversely, the least likely to attend high-quality programs.

Programs Serving Middle-Class Families

When selecting options for their children's care, families in the middle-income bracket might choose public programs, such as preschools in public schools. However, many select private alternatives, such as employer-sponsored, faith-based, family- or home-based, independent, or franchise or corporate child-care centers.

Providers serving the middle-income market segment receive funding from various sources, including parent fees, private contributions, and, in some instances, state funds. Therefore, providers have to coordinate multiple funding streams and regulations from such agencies as the US Department of Education and state child-care departments.

Beginning in the 1970s, corporate chains and franchises figured out that middle-income families were moving to affluent suburbs. As a result, these companies focused their efforts on attracting the clientele in these geographic areas—and the attached annual spending, state funds, and resources. These large companies structured their business plans around the demographic characteristics of this population, including average incomes, age range, and educational backgrounds. Preschools in public school systems, which have more access to infrastructure, resources, and quality improvement plans, also compete for part of this market segment.

Programs Serving High-Income Families

Families in the high-income range prefer to avoid group care during the early years of their children's lives. If they do decide to use group care, they choose providers offering part-time nursery care, home care, or corporate-sponsored programs when available. Because these families are not your primary market segment, this book primarily focuses on attracting low- and middle-income families to your business.

TYPES OF BUSINESS MODELS

New businesses need a plan for how to make money. There are many different business models through which to enter the child-care industry:

- Independent child-care providers

- Home day care

- Faith-based centers and nonprofit chains

- Employer-sponsored care

- Franchises

- Corporate chains

Independent Child-Care Providers

For-profit centers are estimated to constitute more than half of all child-care centers across all ages of children served. Independent providers operate the majority—70 percent—of for-profit centers. According to Yale researchers Laura Stout Sosinsky, Heather Lord, and Edward Zigler, these can range in size and can operate as small, large, or multisite independent centers. They often rely on government subsidies and build a business plan on existing programs or subsidies. These centers vary in terms of market segments and quality. Independent providers are often called "mom-and-pop shops" and pay no fees to be part of a system. Independent child-care providers that serve middle-income families offer distinctive alternatives to parents in their communities and create their brands and support structures to compete in and appeal to the market segment. Nevertheless, they face the disadvantage of competing with franchises and large chains in access to prime real estate locations, economies of scale, curriculum resources, and lack of brand recognition. They do not enjoy the financial savings that come with being part of a network for advertising purposes or purchasing power or a corporate team to support the operations.

Faith-Based Centers and Nonprofit Chains

Even though younger generations are becoming more secular, religiously affiliated preschools are growing. Some nonprofit community organizations, such as the YMCA, provide child care along with the other services they offer. Nonprofit day-care centers usually have a board of directors, and ministries may or may not pay part of the costs.

Nonprofit organizations operate very similarly to for-profit centers but are eligible for grants and other funding and are exempt from state and federal taxes. Nonprofit organizations and worship centers are becoming more aware of the importance of running sustainable child-care centers.

The Sosinsky, Lord, Zigler study from Yale looked at the differences in quality between for-profit and nonprofit child-care centers. They found that nonprofit centers evidenced higher caregiver wages and education, better quality, better child-staff ratios, and lower turnover.

Employer-Sponsored Care

Employers entering the child-care industry want to offer benefits that help them retain key employees, increase productivity, and generate a positive organizational image. Nevertheless, many companies believe that operating child-care centers lies outside their expertise. As researchers Rachel Connelly, Deborah DeGraff, and Rachel Willis describe in their report *Kids at Work*, some employers outsource child-care services to a management company, with the employer providing company vouchers to subsidize part of the child-care costs.

Home Day-Care Centers

Family caregivers tend to attract clients from their social class and are usually considered warmer and homelike. This child-care setting is most popular for infants and toddlers, but such caregivers also cater to preschoolers and children who need after-school care. Some of these caregivers are licensed, depending on the number of children under their supervision, and some programs might be subject to inspections by state authorities.

Franchises

When a child-care company wants to expand into new areas, it may sell franchises. The brand owners are called *franchisors*, and those who buy the rights are called *franchisees*. The franchisor grants a franchisee the rights to use the parent company's brand, name, curriculum, operational systems, and model in a specific territory. In exchange, the franchisee agrees to pay an initial amount of money, a monthly royalty fee, and an advertising fee.

Franchise:
the right or license granted to an individual or group to market a company's goods or services in a particular territory

Some of the best-known child-care franchises started as local success stories whose owners decided to expand. When the owners faced growing pains, such as financing and operating new units, they switched to the franchise model so they could gain the benefits of expansion without having to take on all the responsibility for each new unit. The biggest franchising companies in the child-care industry include brands such as Primrose, Goddard Systems, and the Learning Experience. There is a certain degree of complexity in operating numerous child-care centers in multiple states, with a lot more financial risk involved. For franchisors, selling franchises is a way to minimize the risk and responsibility by passing some of the operational responsibilities to franchisees. The franchisee gains the advantages of a recognized brand, economies of scale, and proven processes without having to start a business from scratch.

Economy of scale:
a proportionate savings in costs gained by an increased level of production (in other words, the more you produce, the less each item costs to produce, and the more of an item you purchase, the less each item costs to buy)

Most child-care brands that operate under a franchise systems compete for potential franchisees with a business background. Some systems require the owner to be present in the operation, and others allow absentee ownership. This business model creates a dual-management system in which owners of the facility handle the day-to-day business of running a center, and the director supervises the education staff.

Corporate Chains

Like franchises, corporate chains operate under one central administration that supervises all the sites. However, in a corporate chain, a central business owns all the locations; there are no independent operators. Corporate chains operate from a centralized location that handles most aspects of the operation, including human resources, accounting, and marketing. The parent company supplies guidelines for fees, advertising, and curriculum. Early childhood corporate chains include Bright Horizons and Kindercare Group.

UNDERSTAND YOUR PARTNERS

Jennifer Grant, the president of the Early Learning Coalition of Seminole County, Florida, brought up a very smart question that serves as a driving question for the chapter: Why should directors interview their owners the same way owners interview their directors?

Abraham Lincoln's famous quote, "A house divided against itself cannot stand," gives us a hint into the secret formula for establishing a thriving child-care center. When advisors, directors, and owners are aligned, the team works together toward a common goal. Empowered directors understand business fundamentals and use that knowledge to choose their employers. Similarly, owners also understand the basics of child development and use their knowledge to navigate the challenges of opening and managing a child-care center.

HOW TO CHOOSE A BUSINESS MODEL

I have been approached by many people over the years on how to open a successful child-care center. Before I respond, I always ask one question: Why do you want to open a child-care business? Author Simon Sinek, in his book *Start with Why: How Great Leaders Inspire Everyone to Take Action*, explains, "People don't buy what you do; they buy why you do it. And what you do simply proves what you believe."

Running a child-care center involves dealing with customers, agencies, employees, parent collections, management, and accounting, while meeting licensing and state requirements. It also involves accepting the responsibility to care for and educate children during the most critical years of development. Your main motivation should be more than just making a living or investing money. Putting Sinek's words into our context: "The children's parents don't buy what you do; they buy why you do it." Your long-term business success is tied to the reputation of your facility. If the right motives are in place, you are on the path to build a business to last. Yet opening a child-care business requires many different skills. It involves your strengths, your financial situation, and developing a business plan.

Choosing a business model is a very personal decision that involves different factors. Think about the following considerations:

- **Your desired level of involvement in the operations:** Do you want to be actively involved in the operation, or would you rather be an investor or absentee owner? Do you have someone you trust to manage the day-to-day operations?

- **Your personal finances:** Do you meet the net-worth requirements of child-care franchises (the average is $500,000)? How much money do you have in savings to start your business? Do you have access to other financing sources?

- **Your professional experience:** Do you feel confident about selling to customers? Do you have experience in business? Are you confident in your leadership capabilities? How do you handle customer complaints? Do you understand your target market? Do you have experience in the industry?

- **Your understanding of child development:** Do you understand the regulations of the child-care industry? Are you passionate about child development? Do you have a backup plan if your director resigns—could you step in?

- **Your community:** Do you need a network of peers to provide advice and moral support on an ongoing basis? Do you have access to prime real estate locations?

- **Your risk tolerance:** How comfortable are you with risk? Are you risk-averse or risk-tolerant? Would you rather follow a proven business model, or are you willing to take some risks?

Depending on your answers, you will realize there are two distinctive, realistic models to follow in the for-profit model: You can be an independent provider, or you can become a franchisee. First, let's briefly look at the pros and cons of each business model, both nonprofit and for profit.

Home Day Care

Home day-care providers are self-employed professionals who run a child-care business out of their homes. This is a great way for early childhood professionals to transition to the business of child care and, in some cases, it offers opportunities to earn more income than would working for a child-care center.

There are advantages to operating a home day care. The initial investment is lower than that of a franchise or an independent child care. There is a built-in marketing differentiator: the homelike environment. A home day care offers better teacher-to-child ratios because there are fewer children per teacher. Usually, the tuition rates are lower than those of franchises or independent child-care centers.

There are also some disadvantages. Running a business out of your home might be a challenge. Marketing, operating, and managing your business by yourself are large tasks. Handling parent fee collections and other aspects of the operation can be a real challenge. Access to a peer support network, curriculum resources, and professional-development opportunities are limited.

Here are some things to think about:

- ☑ Do you meet the state requirements to operate a child-care business in your home?

- ☑ Do you have savings to support the start-up phase of the business?

- ☑ Do you have access to funding sources to finance the operation?

Corporate-Owned Centers

Corporate-owned centers operate multiple centers and are managed under one centralized location. They offer advantages, such as professional-development opportunities through annual conferences, online trainings, and associations; curriculum innovation; higher salaries and benefits as well as career tracks for early childhood professionals; and access to prime real estate locations and real estate experts.

Corporations can provide easier lead generation, branding, and a central corporate office to handle all aspects of the operation, including customer relationship management programs to track customer data.

There are disadvantages as well. You need a considerable amount of net worth to start a corporate chain. This is a capital-intensive model that involves the purchase or lease of real estate assets. Operating multiple units in

Capital: money or assets contributed for a particular purpose, such as starting a company or investing

different territories can be a real challenge. Because most entrepreneurs lack the net-worth requirements of opening corporate-owned centers, this book will focus on other business models.

Nonprofit Chains and Faith-Based Centers

Nonprofit day-care centers are run similarly to independent child-care centers. According to the National Council of Nonprofits, day-care centers and other charitable organizations have a special tax-exempt Internal Revenue Service (IRS) code and limit the amount of compensation they offer for a leadership position.

The advantages of this model are that they are eligible for grants and other funding, and they are exempt from state and federal taxes. Employees are usually compensated better than in other models. They serve diverse communities and market segments and operate at a lower cost to parents.

There are disadvantages as well. Nonprofits are required to be governed by a board of directors. All the money collected from parents and other sources must be invested in the organization. Identifying grants sources might be challenging. Finding a network of peers can be challenging as well. They offer limited curriculum resources and training opportunities for staff members.

Here are some things to consider:

- ▣ Do you feel confident about identifying grant opportunities?

- ▣ Would you prefer a profit-making business?

Like other nonprofits, faith-based programs usually open centers to serve families from diverse backgrounds in different market segments in the local community. They function with the goal of serving others, usually at lower tuition rates for parents. The disadvantages of this model are that it can be challenging to access a peer-support network and curriculum resources; they lack marketing support and branding; and parents might not consider this type of program a high-quality educational offering.

If your religious organization is looking for a way to create a sustainable child-care program, it is advisable to start this process by writing a business plan following the same guidelines of a for-profit business model.

Employer-Sponsored Care

This type of business model requires a provider to sign a contract with an employer. Because few employers offer child-care benefits to employees, we will focus our analysis on other business models. The employer-sponsored model requires highly specialized skills that include contract negotiation with Fortune 500 companies. The market leader in this segment is a company called Bright Horizons, which is listed on the New York Stock Exchange.

Independent Child-Care Providers

Independent providers represent 70 percent of the child-care market. Being an independent provider offers some distinct advantages. You have the opportunity to shape your brand identity and develop your own program guidelines. There is no franchise fee to pay, nor are there any additional fees or royalties, which could represent in some cases up to 10 percent of your total monthly receipts. Should you decide to sell your business in the future, buyers prefer to purchase profitable independent child-care centers, because franchise units often come with more restrictive legal contracts.

Being an independent child-care provider also comes with some disadvantages. Because real estate developers typically prefer to negotiate deals with established brands, child-care brands often have better access than independent providers to prime real estate locations. Funding can also be a challenge. Banks and investors are usually reluctant to lend to inexperienced operators. Independent child-care businesses may pay more for goods and services; franchises can often get goods and services at lower costs by purchasing at group bulk rates. Franchises may have better access to marketing support than independent operators do. Child-care franchises have built their brands over time, making customer lead generation and regional advertising campaigns easier. For an independent child-care operator, it may be difficult to access a network of peers to provide moral support and professional-development opportunities. Independent child-care centers must handle customers themselves; franchises have access to centralized call centers.

Here are some things to think about:

- ▣ Do you have experience in business?

- ▣ Do you have experience in the child-care industry?

- ▣ Do you have leadership capabilities?

- ▣ Are you willing to take more risk and do it yourself?

- ▣ Do you have access to financing sources?

Franchises

If you are more risk-averse and find the idea of starting an independent child-care center a bit daunting, you may wish to purchase a franchise unit. There are some advantages to the franchise model:

- ☑ A network of peers who can offer advice and moral support

- ☑ Professional-development opportunities through annual conferences, online training, and associations

- ☑ A more guided approach to and assistance in securing funding sources

- ☑ Discounts in bulk purchases

- ☑ Proven business model and operational systems

- ☑ Curriculum resources and educational specialists

- ☑ Access to prime real estate locations and real estate experts to guide you through site selection

- ☑ A recognizable brand, marketing support, and easier lead generation

- ☑ Automated customer relationship management to track customer data and measure prospect-to-parent sales processes for enrollment

There are also disadvantages to the franchise model. Franchise fees and other start-up fees can be significant. A *franchise fee* is an initial lump sum payable upon signing the contract. Site-selection fees and development fees refer to assistance offered to help you identify a location. Franchise systems typically require a significant net worth of their franchisees. *Net worth* is the total assets you have (such as your home and cars) minus the amount of money you owe. To qualify for a child-care franchise, you need an average net worth of between $500,000 and $750,000; according to an article published by Daniel Kurt on Investopedia, only 1 percent of the US population meets this requirement. This limits the pool of potential franchisees. As new franchisors enter the market, there are more franchise systems competing to attract the same

Franchise fee: initial lump sum payable upon signing a franchise contract

Net worth: your total assets minus the amount of money you owe

Asset: property owned, such as a building, equipment, or a vehicle

limited pool of ideal candidates. As a result, some franchise systems have become investment vehicles for foreign investors.

Fees Associated with Large Franchises*

FRANCHISE	LICENSE FEE	MINIMUM NET-WORTH REQUIREMENT	ROYALTY FEES	MARKETING FEES
The Learning Experience	$60,000	$500,000	7%	1%
Goddard School	$135,000	$750,000	7%	4%
Primrose Schools	$50,000–$80,000	$350,000	7%	2%

*Fees are current as of the publishing date of this book.

Franchisees pay a considerable amount of gross receipts (up to 10 percent) to the franchise system, and they assume operational risks, must repay loans, and must keep levels of profitability with funding sources. Franchisors may request an audit of any of your franchise's financial statements, at your sole expense, by an independent certified public accountant.

Franchises limit the franchisee's independence, sometimes in unexpected ways. Franchise agreements typically contain restrictive covenants. Once you sign an agreement, you will not be able to open another business in the same industry for the term of the contract while you own the franchise unit. The agreements are signed with fifteen-year terms and are usually renewed every five years thereafter. As a franchisee, you have to follow strict branding guidelines such as the paint colors you use, the promotions that you offer, the curriculum your teachers use, and any remodeling to your unit if the franchisor rebrands.

The reputation of your franchise unit can be affected by the reputation of another franchise unit within the brand. If one unit in a franchise is in trouble, then the entire system is at risk. In Central Florida, for example, a report of child abuse was broadcast at a regional level, putting an entire franchise in jeopardy. In this case, the franchisor had to allow the franchise unit in question to be transferred to a new owner without the franchise agreement.

Not all franchise systems are built to last, and not all franchisors understand that they are transitioning from operators to a support-service company. Franchisors who see their franchisees as their local partners and offer support in operations, training, systems, and marketing are likely to succeed. But as John Stanworth, David Purdy, and Stuart Price explain in their article "Franchise Growth and Failure in the USA and the UK," like any other new start-up, only a small number of franchisors find the magic formula for long-term survival. According to the *Sloane Management Review* article "Factors for New Franchise Success" by Scott Shane and Chester Spell, three-quarters of all new franchise systems fail within twelve years.

Here are some things to think about:

- ▣ Do you meet the net-worth requirement of the franchisor?

- ▣ Are you comfortable with risk, or are you a risk-averse person?

- ▣ Do you lack experience in business management, need access to funding sources, or need more support from a corporate team?

FINDING THE RIGHT FRANCHISE FOR YOU

To avoid getting stuck in a troubled franchise, a potential franchisee should conduct an extensive due-diligence study of each franchise she is considering. Franchising is a highly regulated industry; the federal Franchise Rule (16 CFR Parts 436 and 437) requires that franchises provide potential franchisees the information they need to make an informed decision about the purchase. Franchises must provide prospective franchisees a federally mandated document, called a *franchise disclosure document* (FDD), which must provide information in twenty-three categories and must be updated yearly. You can learn a lot about the credibility of the franchisor by reading the FDDs of at least the last three years. Be sure to review these documents with your attorney.

After reviewing the franchise disclosure documents, conduct initial interviews with prospective franchisors. Be sure to include the following questions:

- » Who is your ideal market?
- » Tell me about your main competitor. How are you different?
- » What are the main challenges of the industry?
- » Tell me about your most successful franchise units. What makes them successful?
- » How many of your units fail every year?
- » Tell me about your failing franchise units. Why do you think they are struggling?
- » What level of support do you provide to prospective franchisees?

- » How will you assist me in identifying funding sources for my project? What is your level of support?

- » Is your franchise system Small Business Administration (SBA) approved or preapproved with any other lender?

- » What level of support do franchisees receive prior to opening for business?

- » What are the initial fees? franchise fee? site-development costs?

- » Do you have potential sites identified in the trade area?

- » What training do you offer?

- » Do you have accreditations in the industry?

- » What is your level of involvement in hiring and recruiting the director of the facility?

- » Who is the person in charge of your education department?

- » What level of support do franchisees receive once they open for business?

- » How do you ensure consistency in the network?

- » Describe your marketing strategy in my region. How many units do you have in my region? How is your marketing fund allocated?

Due diligence:
research and analysis of a company or organization done in preparation for a business transaction

By investing time in the due-diligence period, the franchisee can get a better picture of the system, including the financial strengths of the franchisor, the credibility and business experience of executives of the company, the number of new franchisees in the system, the history of the system, and any legal issues that might be a red flag for an investor.

FOCUSING ON THE FOR-PROFIT MODELS

Over the years, I have been an independent provider, a franchisee, and a franchisor in the child-care industry. Therefore, I understand the challenges of the different for-profit business models.

For my first entrance into the business of child care, I bought a franchise. The main reason for selecting this business model was that, at that time, I lacked experience in the industry, an understanding of real estate criteria, and the capital to purchase a facility. To get started, I needed a proven business model. After some years of operating the unit, I discovered that being part of a franchise system was not the right fit for me. I was not comfortable following all the guidelines of the franchisor, and I did not enjoy the complexities and restrictions of the legal documents.

For my second venture, I became an independent child-care provider. This time I bought a struggling school, but I had established my professional reputation as an operator. I had learned the ins and outs of real estate, the operations, and how to market the program. At the beginning, my banker was hesitant to lend me the funds to purchase a struggling school. Yet my business plan, industry expertise, and arguments convinced the bank to take the risk. With a strong business plan, a marketing differentiator to set my center apart from the competition, and a great team, we were able to turn the center around in less than six months in a market where most of the child-care brands competed for the same clientele. As our waiting list increased, I was intrigued to find out why parents were leaving recognized brands in a highly saturated market.

The "secret sauce" was our marketing differentiator: a strong curriculum and a great team in place. That specific market of highly educated parents was asking more from providers than just a safe place for their children to be during the day. Parents were looking for alternative educational offerings and child-care centers with low staff turnover. Parents wanted a consistent, trained, and caring workforce. For those qualities, they were willing to pay more.

Today, parents are increasingly aware of one of the industry's biggest challenges: the alarming staff-turnover rate. They are asking providers for solutions, as they do not want to see their children transition from one caregiver to the next within the space of a few weeks or months. The only way to deliver high-quality instruction and implement a curriculum is through a stable and trained workforce.

BUILD YOUR KNOWLEDGE

» What are the market segments served by most child-care businesses?

» What is the market share of independent child-care providers?

» What business models do child-care providers use?

» What business model do you think would best suit your needs? Why?

2
BUSINESS-PLAN FUNDAMENTALS

_❝❞_

If you want to reach a goal, you must "see the reaching"
in your own mind before you actually arrive at your goal.

—ZIG ZIGLAR, AMERICAN AUTHOR, SALESMAN,
AND MOTIVATIONAL SPEAKER

MAIN QUESTIONS

» What is a business plan?

» Why is the business plan so important?

» What information should be included in a business plan?

WHY DO SMALL BUSINESSES FAIL?

According to a report from the Small Business Administration, across all industries there are 30.2 million small businesses in the United States employing 58.9 million people. According to "Top 6 Reasons New Businesses Fail" by Michael Deane, about 30 percent of new businesses fail within the first two years; 66 percent fail during the first ten years.

Several factors determine the success or failure of a small business, but it all comes back to the entrepreneur who started the company and her ability to adapt to market changes and demands. Some of the leading causes of failure are lack of a business plan, lack of a marketing plan, insufficient funds or lack of capital, poor management or leadership, a poor location, and bad customer service.

Lack of a Business Plan or Marketing Plan

Child-care owners are typically passionate educators ready to change the world, entrepreneurs willing to invest in the community, or mothers who want to open their homes for a day-care business. Some will succeed while others will fail. Without a solid business plan and a clear understanding of how to market the business, the enterprise will not succeed.

Poor Financial Management

Child-care centers that face economic challenges are easy to spot. They neglect some of the areas of the business or start cutting costs, including reducing the workforce or not buying materials. They struggle to pay bills, pay back a loan, and fulfill other financial commitments. You can be the best leader, but if you lack financial-management skills, your child-care center will fail.

Poor Management or Leadership

People follow leaders. Managers run programs, budgets, constracts, and projects. Some people are excellent managers and poor leaders, while others are great leaders and poor managers. To retain the best employees and operate a profitable center, both competencies are necessary.

Poor Location

According to the website Entrepreneur.com, poor location selection is one of the leading causes of business failures. "Service businesses may not have the foot traffic and high visibility requirements of retailers, but their location has to be convenient for customers, and their employees need adequate parking." The cost of poor real estate selection will be reflected in the revenue your business will generate.

Poor Customer Service

Attaining high levels of customer service in our industry requires a skillful, patient, and seasoned director familiar with responding to common complaints and situations. Let's take as an example the issue of biting incidents among toddlers. Every time there's an incident inside a classroom, a customer complains. Parent reactions can vary from moderate to aggressive. Navigating the parents' emotions and addressing concerns requires a director and staff who can respond with patience and empathy and can implement school protocols consistently.

STARTING A NEW SMALL BUSINESS

Before you greet enthusiastic children and parents at the door, you must lay the foundation for the success of your business. In this preopening or start-up phase, you are incubating the idea. Opening any new center entails risks and a lot of work. The business idea must go through all the steps of the business plan to come to life.

New businesses are exciting, and inexperienced entrepreneurs usually have trouble separating feelings from facts. To determine the feasibility of the project, the entrepreneur has to be able to analyze data and listen to the market without emotions clouding her judgment. Entrepreneurs must be able to set aside their excitement and review their business plans for any flaws that might keep the business from being a success. Solid business plans are based on research, data, and realistic goals. Without proper research, businesses could choose the wrong location or violate licensing regulations.

Start-up:
a new business venture

Throughout my career, I have come up with hundreds of ideas. But only a few of them have survived the first stage of the process: the start-up phase. Usually, it only takes my husband's patience, a glass of wine, a good meal, and the opportunity to listen to myself describe the idea out loud. By the time we finish dinner, most of my ideas have died without his speaking a word. The good ideas, however, won't go away. These are the ideas that merit creating a plan—a business plan.

WHAT IS A BUSINESS PLAN?

Just as architects and engineers draw an architectural plan before building a house, entrepreneurs write business plans to lay the foundation and path for the critical milestones a company must reach upon opening. Business plans help new businesses navigate the process of the start-up phase and lay the groundwork for how the business is going to achieve its goals and overcome obstacles.

I recently sent my last child off to college. Before we headed to campus, Valerie received an extensive email with a reminder of things that we should do before the move, such as items to pack, documents to submit, and meetings to attend. We also created our own to-do lists. Just like the transition to college, your business plan should include a list of things to bring, such as milestones from marketing, financial, and operational perspectives: a marketing plan, budgets, competitor information, and sales projections. The Small Business Administration offers an excellent resource at https://www.sba.gov/sites/default/files/files/pub_mp29.pdf that includes detailed questions to help you understand the information needed to complete a business plan.

Business plan: a document setting out future objectives and strategies for a start-up

When I met Patricia, she had invested all her savings in her new child-care business. But she was struggling to pay expenses and attract new families. A mutual friend asked me if I could help her find out what she was doing wrong.

The first thing I wanted to see was her business plan. By reading the executive summary on the first page, I realized that an industry expert had not developed the plan. Patricia had self-financed the deal; therefore, a lender or an investor had not challenged her business assumptions. The consultant she hired to write the plan recommended that she open a child-care center in an area with an average income level of $150,000 a year and that she lease property close to the most exclusive neighborhood in the city. The space was empty (called a first-generation space), which meant that, to open the business, she had to pay large up-front installation costs for electricity, interior walls, flooring, and restrooms. By looking at the demographic report on the community, I realized that the average income was too high and that there were not many children in the area.

Patricia realized that the initial market research was faulty. She saw young children in the supermarket with their moms and nannies, because some mothers in the *community did not work; that simple fact explained why she did not attract the business of those families. She also learned that some of the parents did not look at group care as a positive experience because of biting incidents or sick care. In addition, many other providers already in the market competed for the same business. The good news from her demographic report was that the market was growing and new communities were being built.*

Since she didn't have a good business plan, Patricia had to think of creative ideas to help her business survive a little longer. One idea we came up with was to target local communities that would fit her desired clientele. She offered new services, such as part-time programs, after-school solutions, and special programs. Luckily, within a couple of years, the market had grown. In a short period of time, her strategies worked, and she now operates a thriving child-care center.

Parts of a Business Plan

A business plan should give the reader specific information about the proposed business. It should include the following:

- ▣ **Executive summary and keys to success**
  - » Company description
  - » Keys to success
  - » Company formation and information about the founders
  - » Owners and shareholders
  - » Location and geographical markets served

- ▣ **Products and services**
  - » Definition of the core products and services
  - » Pricing information

- ▣ **Marketing plan**
  - » Market analysis and market research
  - » SWOT (strengths, weaknesses, opportunities, threats) analysis
  - » Brand and product positioning

- ▣ **Operational plan: Strategy and implementation**
  - » Organization and management team
  - » Founders and executive team
  - » Key team members
  - » Job descriptions

- ▣ **Financial Plan**
  - » Financial projections
  - » Profit and Loss (P and L) statements
  - » Start-up cost expenses

- ▣ **Appendices**

In this chapter, we will examine how to create the first parts of the plan, the executive summary, the company description, and the description of the products and services. We will take a closer look at the other parts in later chapters.

Executive Summary and Keys to Success

Have you heard the saying, "You never get a second chance to make a first impression"? The same principle applies to the business plan. Let's break down some of the information we need to create a powerful opening.

The first section of your business plan is called the *executive summary*. It presents a brief and persuasive description of the reasons someone should be reading your business plan. Usually, an entrepreneur will use the executive summary as an elevator pitch, a brief description of what makes the business unique. Imagine you are taking an elevator with a potential investor or lender. How long do you think the average duration of an elevator ride is? If you can communicate your key idea in twenty to thirty seconds, or two paragraphs, you have a winning formula.

Your executive summary should answer the following questions:

- ▣ What services do we offer?

- ▣ What is our target market?

- ▣ What makes our services unique? What makes us different from our competition?

- ▣ What are our keys to success?

It takes time to develop a powerful elevator pitch and executive summary. The most effective executive summaries include your vision and your mission statement. Your vision is the goal you want to reach at the end of the journey. Your mission statement contains the words to keep you motivated along the route.

> *ABC Learning Center is a community early childhood development program for children ages six weeks to five years and offers after-school care for children ages six to ten years. We are designed to meet the needs of working parents in our*

community by providing first-class child-care services and after-school care. We aim to prepare young learners by offering high-quality curricula taught by certified early childhood professionals.

Next, the executive summary should list your keys to success. These are the standards that will serve as core goals of the program.

ABC Learning Center's Keys to Success:

» *Marketing: A highly customizable child-care center to address the specific needs of our clients*

» *Service quality: Caregiving and educational programs provided by certified educators and child-care workers*

» *Reputation: Maintaining a highly regarded reputation for excellence in caregiving, education, and community involvement*

» *Profitability: Controlling costs and managing budgets in accordance with company goals, adhering to strategic business plans for growth and expansion, and reinvesting in the business and its employees*

Company Description

The next section of the business plan is the company description or the formation. In this section you should include the legal structure of your entity and the ownership interest. Let's start with the basics. Every company has its own legal identity and identification number, called a *federal employer identification number*, or FEIN. Some child-care business owners choose to open two legal entities: one to purchase the real estate and the other to run the operations. By doing so, they are able to reduce certain liability risks in their operation. That means that in the case of a liability claim, the main asset—the real estate— will not be at risk.

The US Small Business Administration website offers great information on how to choose a business structure. https://www.sba.gov/business-guide/launch-your-business/choose-business-structure#section-header-1

Many different legal entities can operate child-care centers: limited liability companies (LLCs), for-profit corporations, and nonprofit organizations. The most common legal structures in our industry are LLCs and for-profit corporations. Consult with a lawyer and certified public accountant (CPA) on how to set up your legal entity and the tax responsibilities of the different legal structures.

In this section you will also introduce the founders of the company and their industry experience. Potential lenders prefer to see owners who have experience in the industry, as the operator of a facility is a key to success for a child-care center.

> *ABC Learning Center operates as a limited liability company. The partners of the entity are Mr. John Smith and Mrs. Cara Smith. Mrs. Smith owns 70 percent of the company shares; an investor owns the remaining shares. Mr. Smith has fifteen years of executive management, marketing, budgeting, and strategic-planning experience. Mrs. Smith holds a director's credential in early childhood education.*

Location and Geographical Markets Served

**BEFORE YOU WRITE
YOUR BUSINESS PLAN**

Before you sit down to write your business plan, you have to identify the ideal site for your business. Selecting the ideal location requires a deep understanding of real estate and your target market preferences. We will discuss real estate in detail in the following chapter, including considerations such as zoning requirements, local taxes, parking spaces, traffic flow, licensing requirements, and health. Child-care centers operate in diverse locations, such as freestanding buildings, strip malls, and homes. Each option represents a different challenge that entrepreneurs will need to overcome.

You may have heard the familiar saying, "What are the three most important factors in choosing real estate? Location, location, location." Location can have a significant impact on the success of your business and is introduced in the first section of the business plan. In this section you will describe the location of your child-care center, including the type of real estate, the square footage of your facility, a general overview of the population, and an analysis of the population characteristics. To write this short paragraph, you will need to conduct research and follow these steps.

1. **Identify your trade area.** Start by targeting your specific market. According to the SBA, the location of the business determines your taxes, zoning laws, and the regulations of your business. Within each area, there are areas that offer growth potential and others that are more established.

The SBA offers useful information on choosing a location at https://www.sba.gov/business-guide/launch-your-business/pick-your-business-location

---

2. **Gather demographic information about the area.** Demographic reports generate data for a one-, three-, or five-mile radius around a location, to help you understand the characteristics of the market. The best way to understand a particular market is by analyzing data reports from the US Census Bureau on that area. The demographic data illustrate a big, comprehensive picture of who lives in an area and information about the average age, income, gender, and marital status of the population. Nonprofit organizations, real estate companies, mapping software, analytics software, chambers of commerce, and universities can also provide helpful information to the entrepreneur during this stage of the process.

RESOURCE TO HELP YOU UNDERSTAND YOUR DEMOGRAPHIC REPORT

The US Census Bureau offers a tool known as the Census Business Builder that can help you conduct market research. Visit https://cbb.census.gov/sbe/# and select "Personal Services" and then "Daycare" in box 1 to get started.

---

3. **Identify potential sites.** Work with a professional commercial real estate agent to identify different potential sites for your child-care facility within your chosen area.

4. **Create a comparison grid.** When you have identified a few possible sites, create a comparison grid of the data for each site. Use the data to narrow down to one site—your optimal site to start the development process.

ABC Learning Center Comparison Grid

PROPERTY	MEETS ZONING REQUIREMENTS	PARKING SPACES	STREET VISIBILITY	PRICE PER SQUARE FOOT	SQUARE FOOTAGE	FREE-STANDING	CONVENIENCE TO CUSTOMERS
Option 1	No	Yes	Yes	$1.50	10,000 sq. ft.	No	Yes
Option 2	Yes	Yes	No	$1.45	8,000 sq. ft.	Yes	Yes
Option 3	Yes	Yes	Yes	$1.85	8,000 sq. ft.	Yes	Yes

ABC Learning Center will operate from option 2 because all criteria for the child-care facility except one, the street visibility, are offered with the property. The location is convenient to customers, the employees have adequate parking, and the price is reasonable. ABC Learning Center intends to overcome the challenge of the street visibility by offering superior service.

BUILD YOUR KNOWLEDGE

Imagine that you have compiled the following demographic report as you conduct market research on a three-mile radius around the site you are considering for your center.

GENERAL DEMOGRAPHICS	2019	PROJECTED 2024
Total population	135,000	145,000
Households	45,000	48,000
Families	34,000	37,000
Average household size	2.6	2.59
Owner-occupied housing units	28,000	32,000

GENERAL DEMOGRAPHICS	2019	PROJECTED 2024
Renter-occupied housing units	17,000	20,000
Median age	36	38
Population by age		
0 to 4 years	3,000	3,500
5 to 9 years	4,000	4,300
Target market information		
Median Household income	$80,000	$85,000
Children enrolled in child care	1,500	1,750

» How many families live in the area?

» What is the median household income?

» How many families own a home?

» How many children ages 0–4 are in the area?

» Is this area growing?

Let's go back to ABC Learning Center to see how they describe their chosen location.

ABC Learning Center offers services to upscale community developments within a three-mile radius of the city of Springfield, Anystate. The demographic profile of the community consists of a median income of $80,000 and a general population of 135,000 people, of whom 2.2 percent are younger than four years old. Our target market is dual-income, middle-income families who value the quality of education. ABC Learning Center is a freestanding structure with an 8,000-square-foot facility with a licensed capacity of 200 children.

You will find more detailed information about the real estate component in chapter X. In the next chapter, we will continue with how to build the marketing section of your business plan.

BUILD YOUR KNOWLEDGE

» Why do you need a business plan?

» Begin writing a draft of your executive summary and keys to success. Don't worry if you don't have all the information now. In later chapters, we will examine how to gather more data to complete it; for now just write what you know.

> What is your vision?
> What is your mission statement?
> What is your elevator pitch?
> What services do you offer?
> What makes your services unique?
> What are your keys to success?

» Write a draft of your company description and include information about the founders and legal entities.

» Write a draft description of the location you will serve.

3

CREATING YOUR MARKET ANALYSIS

_GG_____

Good marketers see consumers as complete human beings with all the dimensions real people have.

—JONAH SACHS, AMERICAN AUTHOR AND ENTREPRENEUR

MAIN QUESTIONS

» Where can you get data on the population in the area you want to serve?

» How can you learn about competitors?

» How do you use the data you collect to choose your market?

Cindy operates a small Montessori school as an independent child-care operator in her community. Her center has served the same neighborhood for generations and continues to show strong financial results. Her building is located on a side street and is twenty years old; the business has managed to survive even with no street visibility. Some strong child-care brands have entered the market—one of them across from her center. As she faces a more competitive landscape, she knows she needs a new marketing plan and strategy. The first thing she does is conduct a parent survey about the things the current parents enjoy the most about her program. The parents tell her that they love the homelike environment and the quality of the education. She also conducts an analysis to understand what makes her stand out from her competitors. What she discovers surprises her: Her center's strengths are actually her competitors' weaknesses. The children who attend her program score higher in standardized-testing scores than the children who attend the other programs. She suddenly remembers her original business plan and part of her initial mission statement: "to provide an enriching and challenging environment where each child is encouraged to develop to his or her fullest potential academically, socially, and emotionally."

Child-care centers operate in a competitive landscape. New centers open their doors across from one another and vie for the same clientele. Some of these centers are thriving, some are surviving, and some are struggling. Many factors contribute to the success of a child-care program, including the location of the facility, the quality of the service, and the needs of the market.

According to the fact sheet "Child Care Families Need More Help to Care for Their Children" by Sarah Jane Glynn, "most children under five years old receive child care from someone other than a parent. Almost one-quarter (23.4 percent) of children under the age of five are in some form of organized child-care arrangement, which includes day-care centers, nurseries, and preschools. The *2019 North American Child Care Sector Benchmark Survey* reports that respondents indicated an average center capacity of ninety-three children.

In the child-care industry, the market need is determined by how many competitors serve the market and whether parents demand the service. Offering a service in an area that doesn't need it is a recipe for failure. When an entrepreneur starts collecting information to find out whether a business idea is viable, he must conduct market research. In simple terms, *market research* consists of gathering information about the community to understand whether the service is needed in that community.

The number of licensed child-care facilities varies by region and state. To determine your market demand, you will need to make a needs assessment of the community where you hope to open a center. Let's say in this sample plan that 25 percent of the children will require child care.

Population from birth to four years old in a three-mile radius: 3,000

3,000 x 25 percent = 750 children need care

The licensed capacity of the child-care centers in the area:
> *Competitor 1: 240*
> *Competitor 2: 200*
> *Total spots in the market: 440*

750 children need care – 440 spots available = 310 market demand

CONDUCTING MARKET RESEARCH: A FIVE-STEP PROCESS

The next part of creating a business plan is the market research, the backbone of developing your marketing plan. The process involves compiling data about the market, the market size, and growth trends; assessing the the competitive landscape; identifying customers' habits; and looking at the results of your market survey. Objective data provides an entrepreneur with the foundation to write a marketing plan, which is how you plan to enter the market.

1. Create your product description.

2. Analyze the competitive landscape.

3. Conduct a SWOT analysis.

4. Conduct a market survey.

5. Describe your brand and service positioning.

Market research: activity of gathering information about consumers' needs and preferences

Create Your Product Description

In this section of the business plan, you can include the description of the different programs you will offer at your center and a brief description of your services. Let's continue with our example.

ABC Learning Center offers child-care services and an innovative curriculum for children ages six weeks to five years. We offer after-school care for children ages six to ten years. Upon its opening, the center will offer:

» *Both full-time and part-time programs:*
  - *Infants*
  - *Toddlers*
  - *Two-year-olds*
  - *Preschoolers*
  - *After school*

Infants, Toddlers, and Two-Year-Olds

Our teachers ensure that babies receive the best care, attention, and opportunities for development. They provide parents with daily communications about their baby's activities and developmental milestones. Our program is designed to support a child's development in the following areas: communication and language, cognitive skills, physical development, and social and emotional development.

Preschoolers

Early preschoolers are guided in making the important transition from individual play to group play. Our early-learning program and curriculum are designed to enhance the physical, socioemotional, language, and cognitive development of each child.

After School

We accept children ages six to ten years in our after-school program, providing special activities and assistance with homework.

Analyze the Competitive Landscape

Once you narrow down the services you want to offer, the second step of the process is understanding your competition. Understanding your competitive landscape will allow you to have a better picture of the market. You might find out that you have different competitors in your market, but not all of them are targeting the same ideal customers. Those ideal customers should be the primary target market of your business.

As a child-care provider, you will not be able to meet the needs and wants of your entire market. Some families are looking for providers that they can afford. Others are seeking specific educational programs or lower teacher-to-child ratios. By identifying the market that aligns best with your strengths, you start identifying your ideal customer.

Before you even start offering your service, the first thing you need to understand is whom you are helping. The specific group of people you intend to help is called your *target market*, your ideal customers of a certain age, gender, and income level. In the ABC Learning Center example, the target market is dual-income families, meaning that both parents work outside the home, who earn an average household income of $80,000.

As you find out more about your market you will start to discover different "buyer personas" or different types of parents. You have to make an intentional decision on the families you want to serve. For example, we once received a parent inquiry over the phone. We invited the parent to come in for a tour, but she insisted on knowing the price prior to the visit. She told the director how much she was paying and asked if we could match it. We kindly told her that we were not able to do that and referred her to a competitor. Why would we do that? Because she did not match our buyer persona. She was looking for a discounted service. We are looking for parents who value our services and are willing to pay a fair price.

As you find out about your competitors, you will learn that there are direct competitors and secondary competitors that offer a higher or lower end of your service within the same geographical area. By categorizing your competitors into different levels, you can narrow down the research and discover which competitors are targeting your same ideal customers. Centers that are targeting the same audience will have a similar level of services and similar prices. In the same way, secondary competitors offer child-care services to another target customer in the same geographical area and typically will compete by offering lower or higher prices and a different quality of service.

Gather information about your direct and secondary competitors, and create a competitor grid. A *competitor grid* is a graph that helps you analyze information about the companies and service providers in your area—your competitive landscape. You can learn a lot by visiting your competitors' websites and researching online communities. You can find out their prices, primary target market, and what makes them unique.

Competitor grid:
a graph that helps you analyze information about the companies and service providers in your area

John Smith and Cara Smith, owners of ABC Learning Center, start by gathering each competitor's price information per age group and obtaining important data such as each center's licensed capacity. They focus on competitors within a three-mile radius of their chosen location.

Licensed capacity:
The total number of children in care allowed in a facility

Competitor Grid of Enrollment in a Middle-Income Area

	ABC LEARNING CENTER	COMPETITOR #1	COMPETITOR #2
INFANTS	$270	$290	$290
YOUNG TODDLERS	$260	$260	$270
TODDLERS	$220	$250	$260
PRESCHOOLERS	$240	$230	$250
PREKINDERGARTNERS	$230	$230	$200
AFTER-SCHOOL CHILDREN	$75	$90	$93
LICENSED CAPACITY	200	220	220
WAITING LIST	n/a	YES	YES

As you compile your list of competitors, you may discover that there are more competitors than there are children to fill the centers. This is called *market saturation*. If your market is full of competitors, there are some strategies you can use to survive and thrive.

- ▣ Take enrollments from your competitors by lowering your prices.

- ▣ Offer better service, such as later hours, after-school care, curriculum, and other options.

- ▣ Offer discounts, vouchers, or promotions.

Child-care centers that thrive in a saturated market have a realistic understanding of what makes them stand out. Those qualities that make a business unique are the *market differentiators*. However, even if you have strong market differentiators, sometimes a market is so saturated that starting a new child-care center in that area would be a bad idea. For instance, I once visited some sites in Texas for a specific trade area. I looked at the competitor grid and found out that every competitor was located within a mile of each other and offered very similar services. On top of that, all of them had many spaces available. When direct competitors offer more spaces than the local demand needs, it is probably a good idea to find a new trade area.

Market saturation:
a situation in which there are more providers of goods or services than there is a demand for those goods or services

Direct competitor:
service provider who offers similar services. Your direct competitors are targeting the same clientele as you are. Because you are not able to meet the demands across your market, focus on your buyer persona and your direct competitors.

Secondary competitor:
service provider who offers services in the same geographic area, but at different levels of quality and price

Next, the Smiths look at how their competitors stack up against ABC Learning Center in quality, price, and location. With this information, they are able to identify their direct and indirect competitors within the three-mile radius.

Competitor Grid for ABC Learning Center

COMPETITOR	LOCATION	CONSTRUCTION	PRICES	QUALITY	LICENSED CAPACITY	TYPE OF COMPETITOR
Primrose	Free standing	1985	Similar	Similar	200	Direct
Learning Experience	Free standing	2018	Similar	Similar	160	Direct
Little Angels	Strip mall	n/a	Lower	Lower	100	Indirect
Kindercare	Free standing	1970	Lower	n/a	120	Indirect

Conduct a SWOT Analysis

This step of the process also includes developing your SWOT analysis. SWOT stands for strengths, weaknesses, opportunities, and threats. A SWOT analysis is a tool to help you develop your marketing. Understanding your SWOT analysis helps you identify your top strengths and your marketing differentiators and compare them to those of your competitors. Your SWOT analysis could also help you determine your price point.

SWOT Analysis for ABC Learning Center

COMPETITOR	STRENGTHS	WEAKNESSES	OPPORTUNITIES	THREATS
ABC Learning Center	• Innovative curriculum • New state-of-the-art facility • New computer lab • Owner-operated facility; owner is also the director • Director with a successful track record • Lower staff-to-child ratios	• Location (inside the community) • Independent provider with a limited marketing budget	• Could accept funding from government • Could partner with businesses in the area to subsidize care • Could allocate local marketing budget for sponsorships	• Increased competition • Employers are creating in-house centers • Economy
Competitor #1	• Prime real estate; better location • Franchise—has monthly marketing investment allocated	• School-readiness scores are low • Building is not remodeled • Doesn't have great customer service • Leadership struggles; has had two directors in the last year • High staff-to-child ratios	• Could remodel the facility • Could hire a new director	• Increased competition • New administration taking over • Economy is struggling

COMPETITOR	STRENGTHS	WEAKNESSES	OPPORTUNITIES	THREATS
Competitor #2	• Near the public elementary schools in the area • Outstanding reputation in the local community • Franchise with an allocated marketing budget • Good school-readiness scores	• Building is not remodeled • High prices • Higher staff-to-child ratios	• Could update facility • Could hire staff to decrease ratios	• Increased competition • Economy is struggling

All businesses are at risk of decline or death. New, beautiful child-care centers with better differentiators could enter your market, and you might no longer have a competitive advantage. Keeping up with market trends and reinvesting in staff allows companies to stay ahead of the competition. By identifying your weaknesses and threats, you can find solutions to those challenges prior to opening your center.

Conduct a Market Survey

Before opening my first center, I spent years conducting informal market research. When my children started school, one of my priorities was to stay close to them because I didn't want to spend a long time commuting back and forth to work. I knew some parents in the community, so the best way to find out if the project was feasible was to start asking potential customers the right questions.

There are many ways to conduct market research in the age of social media, including sending out a survey to parents, joining an online community to learn more about the needs of parents in your area, or attending a community event and asking parents for input.

My list of questions included some of the following:

1. How often do you need child care?

2. How much do you pay?

3. Can you recommend a good program? Why do you like it?

4. What are parents recommending in online communities?

Asking questions of potential customers is called a *market survey*. Entrepreneurs who remain objective during this phase of the process can separate emotions and personal interests from real data. A market survey helps entrepreneurs understand the spending characteristics of the population— data that are essential for preparing a reasonable income forecast. Conducting market research might not always lead to the expected results but will lay the foundation of a strong marketing plan for the long run.

Market survey: research and analysis of a market for a particular product or service, including an investigation into consumer preferences

In my case, after asking questions of other parents in the community, I compiled information that I didn't like. I realized that the service I had in mind was not going to provide the expected revenues to support an income forecast for a long-term business plan. The market was saturated; there were just too many competitors vying for the same pool of customers. I realized that every other brand was present in that market and that the franchise I wanted to buy did not have a strong differentiator. Furthermore, there were not a lot of new parents moving into that area, and in most instances at least one of the parents could afford to stay at home with the children. I realized that the market was not the ideal place to build a twenty-year business plan, so I ended up commuting to work two hours every day because I wanted to be in a trade area with more population growth. More than a decade later, my research and assumptions proved to be right. The market I did end up choosing grew 5 percent every year, reflecting the fact that more families were moving into the area. Building a school in the right market sets the foundation for long-term success.

Successful marketing research leads to three potential outcomes: Yes, No, or Maybe Later. A *yes* market would be a growing population of young families, many competitors with families on waiting lists, and a strong product with a great marketing differentiator. A *no* market would be a saturated market with too many competitors with available slots in their programs or a lack of a demographic profile (young families, lots of children, parents who work outside the home and need child care) to support opening a business there. Some markets might be premature markets; that is often the case with new housing developments. If your demographic report indicates strong population growth and new residential developments, but the market does not have a minimum population yet, that would be a *maybe later*.

Some time after opening my first child-care center, I opened my first franchised school in the middle of a recession, with only twenty-five children enrolled and eight staff members. My budget did not allow me to hire a director, so I had to become not only the owner but also a lead teacher and operator of the facility. The first two years were challenging in terms of cash flow. I operated in what I call "emergency mode" at all times: a skeleton crew and I worked twelve-hour shifts.

I was barely making it until I decided to challenge my franchisor's business model. I learned very early on that buying a franchise in the industry didn't guarantee success or support. In the end, it would be my financial loss if things went under. I pulled out my business background, determined to understand the market and adjust to market demands.

During that time, many parents had lost their jobs, and they were barely able to make ends meet each week. The reality was that our program was expensive and did not accept income from government funding sources. I conducted a survey in the community to better understand their needs. When the results came back, I adjusted to the market conditions and introduced new part-time programs so parents could have child care while they went to interviews for new jobs. I also started accepting new funding sources for lower-income families. The lessons I learned from my experience were to be responsive to my market and to be responsible for my own destiny.

BUILD YOUR KNOWLEDGE

Conduct a market survey in the area where you want to locate your business. Ask questions such as the following:

» Do you need child-care services?

» What types of services do you need? part-time? full-time? half-day?

» What is the most important thing for you when choosing a provider? safety? curriculum? teachers? low child-to-staff ratios?

» How much do you pay or are you willing to pay for your services?

Keep your survey short and simple. You will get a wealth of information on your specific market.

Develop Your Brand and Service Positioning

Once your demographic and marketing research is completed, you are ready to develop your brand and service positioning. This is how you intend to compete in the market with a strong differentiator.

From the SWOT analysis, the Smiths can identify ABC Learning Center's marketing differentiator and the ideal customer they are targeting. In this case, their strengths are the competitors' weaknesses. That's what will make ABC Learning Center stand out.

Strengths

- » *Innovative curriculum*
- » *State-of-the-art facility*
- » *New computer lab*
- » *Owner-operated school*
- » *Lower staff-to-child ratio*
- » *Education tailored to achieve high school-readiness scores*

BUILD YOUR KNOWLEDGE

Look back at the demographic report on pages 26 and 27. Then look at the information in the competitor grid of enrollment on page 34. By analyzing the competitor grid, you can identify whether a market is saturated or when the potential market demand is a negative number and there is no market growth. In this case, there is a population of children who may need care.

Number of children in a three-mile area under the age of four years: 3,000

Number of children attending child care in that area (25 percent):
3000 x .25 = 750

Total licensed capacity of child-care centers in the area:
440 (competitor #1 + competitor #2)

Potential market demand: 310

HOW IS LICENSED CAPACITY DETERMINED?

The licensed capacity of a child-care program is determined by the state licensing authority using the following factors*:

» Indoor floor space square footage

» Outdoor square footage

» Sewer/septic capacity (as determined by the health department)

» Number of toilets and wash basins

Licensed capacity is determined by which of these factors is the smallest. For example, if a center has enough indoor and outdoor square footage to accommodate 250 children but only enough sewer/septic capacity to accommodate 200 children, then the licensed capacity would be 200. The licensed capacity must be posted conspicuously in the center.

*These are the requirements in Florida. Your state requirements may vary.

Target market:
the potential buyers in the area who are most likely to need your services

Positioning:
market survey results showing how your target market perceives the child care in your area; this will help you create branding and marketing messages

Market differentiator:
SWOT analysis and a description of how your program is different from the competition

Marketing strategy:
plan to achieve your sales goals, your marketing budget, and a general overview of the marketing mix you intend to use

Let's take a look at the ABC Learning Center brand-positioning statement.

Target market: Our target market is dual-income families with children younger than the age of ten, with an average household income of $80,000 a year. Because both parents work, they do not have time to raise their children during the day. Parents are looking for programs with higher curriculum quality. The market need for higher quality child care is stronger than ever. According to the US Census Bureau, the community will grow by 6 percent over the next five years.

Brand-positioning statement: There are ten early childhood programs in the community, but only two centers are located within the three-mile target radius. Competitor 1 and Competitor 2 target our same customers and have a combined license capacity of 440, which translates into a market need of a remaining 310 spots. We will position ABC Learning Center as a safe, nurturing environment with an innovative curriculum operated by an owner/director.

Marketing differentiator: The competitive advantage of ABC Learning Center is that we compete with a state-of-the-art facility, a new computer lab, an innovative curriculum, and first-class child-care services operated by an owner/operator. We intend to overcome the challenge of the location of the real estate by offering superior customer service and investing in a sign to help prospective customers identify our location.

Our opportunities include accepting government vouchers from the X program, partnering with local business, and a local marketing budget.

Marketing goals:

» Position ABC Learning Center as the premier child-care facility in our community.

» Enroll 110 children in the first year of operations and be at full capacity by the second year.

» Build customer loyalty through superior service and a high-quality educational program.

» Increase the referral rate by 5 percent per quarter.

BUILD YOUR KNOWLEDGE

1. Begin compiling your market-research data. First, look at the area where you would like to start a center.

   - What is the size of your market?
   - What is the demographic profile for that market?
   - How many children younger than age five are in that market?
   - What is your target market? Look at the median household income for the area.

2. Next, take a look at the potential for market growth.

   - Who are your competitors?
   - What is the total licensed capacity in the market? Look at the other centers and gather what their licensed capacities are.
   - What would your licensed capacity be?
   - What is the difference between the number of young children in the area and the total licensed capacity? Is there room for growth, or is this market saturated?

3. What barriers do you face to entering your market? For example, is real estate difficult to purchase? Are the prime locations already taken?

4. Conduct a SWOT analysis.

   - What are your strengths?
   - What are your weaknesses?
   - What are your opportunities?
   - What are your threats?

5. Conduct a market survey.

   - What are your potential customers looking for?
   - How can you differentiate your center from the competition?

4
PUTTING TOGETHER A FINANCIAL PLAN AND PROJECTIONS

_____ 66 _____

Our goals can only be reached through a vehicle of a plan in which we must fervently believe, and upon which we must vigorously act. There is no other route to success.

—PABLO PICASSO, ARTIST

MAIN QUESTIONS

» How do you determine how much money you will need to start?

» How do you identify your real estate site?

» How do you develop your sales projection?

» How do you create a start-up cost estimate?

» How do you create a cash flow analysis?

» How do you build a profit and loss statement?

Mrs. Carla was one of the best teachers at my first school. She had a dynamic personality, a kind heart, and leadership skills. After years of experience working as a lead teacher, she declined a position as an assistant director to start her child-care center. She emptied her savings account and convinced family members to invest in her dream. She found a perfect space close to her home. The real estate offering inside a strip mall was strategically located next to a supermarket.

She quickly learned that there were many different aspects and players involved in the early stages of the process that had nothing to do with education, and she was forced to learn a new set of skills including negotiating lease agreements with landlords, making budgets, recruiting teachers, and getting a license. She had negotiated the lease at an unfavorable price with only a couple of months of grace period to remodel. After signing the contract, she started rebuilding the unit, adding cabinets, bathrooms, and flooring. Just a few weeks into the project, she realized that the remodeling company had miscalculated some costs; the remodel ended up being almost double her initial budget. She waited months for the fire department to inspect the facility. When they finally came, they required additional changes to get the building approved for the final inspection. When she received her certificate of occupancy, she was ready to apply for her provider's license.

Cash reserves:
money a company or individual keeps on hand to meet short-term and emergency funding needs

She unpacked her brand-new inventory and, with the help of her newly hired staff, set up the classrooms in preparation for the final inspection. There was just one thing missing: her license. She went in person to the department to request a site visit, but they kindly directed her to the regulations handbook and reminded her that they had up to forty-five days to conduct the initial appointment. The team waited for days for the inspector to come. During the process, they gave a few tours to prospective parents and rearranged the classrooms. When the inspector finally arrived, they had to wait a few more weeks for the department supervisors to approve the license.

Just a few months after opening, she started facing some significant challenges. She was not able to enroll the number of children needed to cover her expenses, and she was running out of cash reserves. She had to choose between paying her staff, the electrical bill, or the rent; she decided not to pay her rent. Within a few months, her landlord sued her for lack of payment, and she had only a few days to vacate the premises. The center closed down, and a talented director lost her life savings.

Working without a business strategy is like driving your car without a map or a navigation system. It's a great way to get lost and never reach your intended destination. Like all disciplines, business and finance have a unique vocabulary. When directors and entrepreneurs become familiar with this new vocabulary, they can overcome the fear of the unknown and demystify the financial part of the operation. So let's get started with the basics.

All companies start with an idea. With research, planning, and hard work, the idea blossoms into a business. The riskiest stage of the process is the beginning. During this phase, the entrepreneur needs information, objectivity, planning—and money. Bankers are often nervous about making loans to new businesses, especially child-care providers. Prospective owners typically walk with enthusiasm into a banker's office to request start-up capital, but the reality is that most of them receive a rejection letter in the mail a few days later. From a lender's perspective, start-up companies are a risky investment, especially when prospective owners lack experience in the industry. That is one of the reasons some entrepreneurs choose to buy franchises with a proven track record of success. That said, there are several steps you should take prior to your first visit to a bank to request a bank loan.

BUILDING YOUR FINANCIAL STATEMENT

Find your location. Determine whether you will buy, lease, or build to suit your location. You need this information to determine the following, which are parts of your financial statement:

- Your start-up budget

- Your down payment and funding sources

- Your profit and cost projections

Identify the Real Estate Site

Once you identify the area where you want to open your business, the most difficult part of the process begins: identifying the real estate site. To create your financial projections, you must identify the ideal site for your business. Identifying the perfect location requires a level of expertise in commercial real estate, so you will need to work with an experienced commercial real estate agent. There are several ways to acquire a site:

- ▣ Build to suit

- ▣ Lease agreement

- ▣ Repurpose real estate

- ▣ Purchase land and develop your project

- ▣ Purchase an existing center

Building to Suit

If you decide to use this approach, a developer will build the facility for you, and then you will lease it for a specific term. Most real estate developers prefer to work with established brands in exchange for corporate guarantees, which means that the franchisor will act as a guarantor in the lease agreement in the event that the franchisee is not able to meet her obligations. That is the main reason some established brands have an advantage over independent providers to access prime real estate locations.

There are pros and cons to this approach. The pros are that it requires a lower down payment for the total cost of the project, as there is not a real estate acquisition involved, and you can develop a new facility that meets your specific requirements.

The cons are that, because child-care centers are considered a risky business and the success of the unit depends on the operator of the facility, landlords and developers might require personal guarantees, higher cap rates, higher deposits, and collaterals to protect their investments. Developers and build-to-suit partners do not hold the real estate asset for a long period of time, so they will sell the lease to another real estate investor, which means that you will probably pay higher rent.

Signing a Lease Agreement

Real estate developers usually prefer to negotiate with the established brands and require deposits and corporate or personal guarantees. Lease agreements typically have fifteen-year terms with renewal periods. The agreements often include terms such as the following:

- ▣ **Incidental expenses:** These are costs on top of your base rent. They may include property taxes, repairs, insurance, maintenance fees, and common-area maintenance fees.

- ▣ **Common-area maintenance:** Tenants usually share common costs such as landscaping and property management.

- **Triple net lease:** In this type of lease, you pay the rent plus the property taxes, insurance, and maintenance costs.

- **Tenant improvement allowance:** This is the cash amount offered by the landlord to help pay for some of the costs of the renovations.

The pros of a lease agreement are that the total project cost will require a lower down payment, as you are not purchasing a real estate asset and the landlord might also offer a tenant improvement allowance to help pay for the cost of renovations.

The con is that a lease agreement requires a personal guarantee of payment.

The good news is that, because consumers prefer to make purchases online, the real estate market is undergoing a transformation in the age of the digital economy. Child care is still one of the very few businesses that need real estate, and this trend will shift the advantage to independent child-care providers, as real estate developers and mall owners must figure out how to repurpose their developments with the intent to fill vacant spaces.

Repurposing Real Estate

Repurposing is changing the original purpose of intended use. This would include free-standing buildings, strip malls, or spaces inside malls that have not been used as child-care centers, such as a former drugstore or shoe outlet. The space would have to meet the zoning and space requirements of your state licensing agency to be repurposed as a child-care center.

The pro of this approach is that the building is already built and might meet the licensing regulations requirements. The con is that remodeling costs might be prohibitively expensive.

Building Your Center

In this model, the center owner purchases the real estate and builds the facility. Developing a new site for a child-care center requires real estate development expertise because it involves feasibility studies, site investigation reports, and research. Market demand is shifting to new communities where young families are moving, so this type of real estate offers an opportunity. Franchisors usually require franchisees to build within precise parameters, including specific square footage, number of classrooms, and licensed capacity. In this scenario you will have to purchase the land, develop the project, and build your building.

The pros of this approach are the tax advantages that you can get in some states, such as property-tax deductions and depreciation. Usually, banks have more favorable interest rates for this model, called an *owner-operator model*. The cons are that you will be required to pay a higher down payment than you would by purchasing an existing center, and you will have a much larger loan, as the real estate will represent the largest portion of your investment. Because you are building, you will have to wait a couple of years for your new school to open. You will have high up-front costs and will have to make personal guarantees to ensure that the loan is repaid.

BUILD YOUR KNOWLEDGE

Assume that you are making a 20 percent down payment. Purchasing real estate can cost around $1,000,000. Further, setting up the business can cost in the area of $200,000.

$1,000,000 + $200,000 = $1,200,000 (personal capital plus a loan).

Twenty percent of $1,200,000 = $240,000 down payment (the amount of personal capital you would need).

On the other hand, building to suit or leasing a property and setting up the business would require about $200,000 (personal capital plus a loan).

Twenty percent of $200,000 = $40,000 (the amount of personal capital you would need).

Purchasing an Existing Center

This approach involves analyzing the financial statements of the business to be acquired and the valuation of the business based on the level of profitability of the center. The pros of this approach are that you would be purchasing an already-running business that is generating profits, which would make it easier to get financing. You also would not have to deal with real estate selection; that part has already been done. The cons are that profitable centers are expensive and might not be for sale in the area where you want to be, and transitioning to new management is difficult for employees.

Mortgage or rent payments can be costly. Some child-care centers and franchisees enter into unfavorable and expensive rental agreements that put them at risk over time. After conducting a market study and selecting a location, make sure to compare the price per square foot in the area. Study the market objectively with independent commercial real estate professionals who can provide you with comparable properties to help you make an informed decision.

When purchasing an existing center, you have to consider the demographic profile of the community. As communities mature, the population tends to move to new areas and the market demand changes. You might find a child-care building in the wrong demographic area. For example, my husband and I live in an established community with an average population age of forty-five years. New families are not moving into this area. Because the area is not growing, offering child-care services to this community might not be a great idea.

Build Your Start-up Budget

Once you have identified your site, you are ready to create your start-up budget—how much money you will need to open for business. This is the time to start requesting quotes from different vendors for the supplies you will need, then use that information to help you figure out your start-up investment cost. Consider the following fees and purchasing costs as you build your budget. (Note: This is not a comprehensive list, but it will get you started on making your own list.)

- **Furniture:** computers, desks, tables, chairs, high chairs, shelves, storage cabinets, cubbies, changing tables, dramatic-play furniture

- **Toys and materials:** blocks, art-exploration materials, dramatic-play clothes and materials, musical instruments, dolls, riding toys, balls, puzzles, math manipulatives, games, children's books, puppets, fine-motor toys, software, cleaning equipment

- **Playground:** climbing structures, slides, swings, sandboxes, water tables, shade structures, trashcans, benches, tables, fall-zone surface material

- **Insurance:** child-care liability and injury, general liability, property, workers' compensation, commercial auto

- **Marketing:** website development, advertising

- **Security deposits:** utilities

- **Licensing:** inspections and registration with the city or tax collector's office

- **Preoperating expenses:** consultants, legal fees to open your legal entities, inspections, and permits

- **Operations budget:** preopening payroll, job listings, criminal background screenings, health screenings, trainings, and so on

Let's go back to ABC Learning Center. They have identified a property for lease and have contacted the landlord to ask for lease terms. The landlord has asked ABC to complete a lease application that includes personal financial statements and a credit application. A few days later, the landlord comes back with the following lease conditions:

- » *Term: Lease term of 15 years with five-year renewals*
- » *Guarantors: Mr. and Mrs. Smith*
- » *Deposit: $40,000*
- » *Tenant allowance: The landlord will give a tenant allowance of up to $50,000 for renovations.*

Gross leaseable area (GLA): the size in square feet of the premises

The rent schedule is as follows:

LEASE YEAR	ANNUAL MINIMUM RENT	MONTHLY INSTALLMENTS	RATE PER GLA PER YEAR
1	$150,000	$12,500	$12.50
2	$150,000	$12,500	$12.50
3	$174,000	$14,500	$14.50
4	$174,000	$14,500	$14.50
5	$174,000	$14,500	$14.50
6	$191,400	$15,950	$15.95
7	$191,400	$15,950	$15.95
8	$191,400	$15,950	$15.95
9	$191,400	$15,950	$15.95
10	$191,400	$15,950	$15.95
11	$210,540	$17,545	$17.55

LEASE YEAR	ANNUAL MINIMUM RENT	MONTHLY INSTALLMENTS	RATE PER GLA PER YEAR
12	$210,540	$17,545	$17.55
13	$210,540	$17,545	$17.55
14	$210,540	$17,545	$17.55
15	$210,540	$17,545	$17.55

By now, Mr. Smith has requested quotes from the different vendors. With that information and with the real estate information associated with the project, the Smiths can create their first start-up cost budget.

START-UP COSTS	BUDGET
Real estate deposit and guarantees	$40,000
Utility deposits	$5,000–$10,000
School equipment and supplies	$50,000–$60,000
Playground equipment	$30,000
Insurance	$3,000–$5,000
Initial marketing budget	$20,000
Licenses	$2,000
Software	$1,000
Bank fees for loan processing	$4,000
Additional contingency funds (3 months)	$50,000
Legal fees	$3,000
Training	$2,000
Electricity/telephone	$1,000
Build-out/renovations	$10,000
Total	**$221,000–$238,000**

Determine Your Financial Contribution

Next, you will need to determine your own financial contribution, your down payment. Ideally, the bank will want to see a down payment that ranges from 15 percent to 20 percent of the total project cost, as well as the sources of that money. From the previous example, we estimate that ABC Learning Center will require from $221,000 to $238,000 to get started. That means the owners will need 20 percent of that amount—or between

$44,200 and $47,600—for the down payment. I also recommend having a contingency of at least 10 percent of your personal contribution, to meet unexpected expenses. In this case, that would be between $4,420 and $4,800.

Mr. and Mrs. Smith have decided that they will gather the money for their down payment from a few different sources: personal savings, a loan from a relative, and an angel investor. ABC Learning Center is looking for an investor to purchase 30 percent of the shares. They are also signing a note from a relative for $5,300 at a 7 percent annual rate. The note will be paid in full in two years. With these funds, they will have a down payment and contingency.

Angel investor:
someone who invests personal money in a new company

Contingency:
a provision for a potential adverse event, such as a lawsuit

SOURCE	SHARES	AMOUNT
Personal savings	60 percent	$31,800
Note from relative at 7 percent interest	10 percent	$5,300
Investor	30 percent	$15,900
Total	**100 percent**	**$53,000**

Decide on the Funding to Apply For

Next, consider the type of funding you would like to apply for. Several types of funding are available: Small Business Administration (SBA) loans, commercial loans, and lines of credit.

SBA Loans

According to Fundera, Inc., a funding resource for small businesses, "SBA loans are business loans guaranteed by the Small Business Administration. With their multiple SBA funding programs, this government agency provides SBA loan guarantees of up to 85 percent of the loan amount provided through an SBA-approved lender—typically banks. The three main SBA loan programs let you borrow money for nearly any business purpose, including working capital, purchasing inventory or equipment, refinancing other debts, or buying real estate, through these SBA-guaranteed loans."

Commercial Loans

A commercial loan, according to Investopedia.com, is a debt-based funding arrangement between a business and a financial institution such as a bank. It is used to fund capital expenditures and/or cover operational costs that the company may otherwise be unable to afford.

Lines of Credit

A credit line is a funding tool extended by a bank that enables the customer to draw on the funding when needed. The line of credit will offer funding up to an agreed-upon amount, but the customer may withdraw only as much money as is necessary to meet expenses. The customer will then be expected to repay that amount with interest. The line of credit is similar to a credit card, except the line of credit typically has a much lower rate of interest and a higher credit limit available to the customer.

Once you have an idea of your initial start-up costs and your funding sources, you will need to develop your profit and loss projections.

Developing Projections

Managing a company is like running a household. As part of the business plan, a company prepares a budget that estimates how much money the center is going to generate and how much it is going to spend. To start building your projections, you need to include specific projections of revenue and expenses. To do that, you will need to take the following steps.

- ▣ Calculate your average monthly tuition.

- ▣ Forecast your revenue based on sales projections.

- ▣ Calculate your expenditures.

- ▣ Develop your cash flow statement.

Calculate the Average Monthly Tuition

The first step is to calculate the blended tuition average. The *blended tuition average* is the sum of all the tuition plans divided by the total number of programs offered; calculating the blended tuition simplifies creating the financial statements.

As an example, look back at the Competitor Grid of Enrollment in a Middle-Income Area on page 34 for the tuition prices that ABC Learning Center will charge. Add the tuition cost for each age group and program:

$270 + $260 + $220 + $240 + $230 + $75 = $1,295

Find the blended average by dividing that total by the number of programs. There are five full-time programs and one part-time program. $1,295 / 6 = $215.83 or (round up) $216. This number is the average of all the tuitions at the center.

Next, use the blended tuition average to calculate the average yearly tuition rate per student.

Find the yearly tuition average for ABC Learning Center by multiplying the blended tuition average by fifty-two (the number of weeks in a year):
$216 x 52 = $11,232

Then, calculate the average monthly tuition. To do that, divide the yearly tuition average by twelve months.

For ABC Learning Center, divide the yearly tuition average by twelve:
$11,232 / 12 = $936

Forecast Revenue Based on Sales Projections

Preparing a sales forecast is tricky, as you have to predict how many children will enroll in your center within a period of time. Business plans usually include a sales projection that starts low and increases gradually. To build this, you will need to make some assumptions.

ABC Learning Center is planning to open in January with thirty children enrolled. It expects to enroll eighty additional children over the course of the first year. By the end of the first fiscal year (January to December), the owners project that they will have 110 children registered. Multiply the total number of children enrolled each month by the average monthly tuition of $936.

MONTH	NEW ENROLLMENTS	TOTAL ENROLLMENT	TOTAL TUITION
January	30	30	$28,080
February	10	40	$37,440
March	10	50	$46,800
April	10	60	$56,160
May	0	60	$56,160
June	10	70	$65,520
July	10	80	$74,880
August	10	90	$84,240
September	10	100	$93,600
October	10	110	$102,960
November	0	110	$102,960
December	0	110	$102,960

ABC Learning Center's sales projection at the end of the first year is $851,760.

Calculate Expenditures

Now that you have an idea of your revenue, you can figure out how much money you are going to spend. To organize the expenditures, accountants create an accounting chart that might include some sub-accounts. In a child-care setting, labor is the most expensive cost of business, followed by cost of renting the facility. To simplify the budget, we will consider the revenue and the expense sections. Your operational expenses include administrative costs such as payroll, taxes, mortgage or rent, marketing, and professional services. They can also include membership fees, field trips, and other costs.

☐ **Insurance:** You will need different types of coverage to protect the business, such as:

» **Child-care liability insurance** and **child-care accident insurance:** protect the business from the costs of accidents and injuries

» **General liability insurance:** a part of the general insurance system of risk financing to protect the purchaser from the threats of liabilities imposed by lawsuits and similar claims

» **Workers' compensation insurance:** protects your employees and your business from the costs of work-related accidents

» **Property insurance:** provides protection against most risks to property, such as fire, theft, and some weather damage

▣ **Payroll** is one of the most substantial expenses in your center. Understanding payroll requires a deep understanding of operations, scheduling, rules, and regulations. We will look more closely at this topic in a later book.

▣ **Professional services:** include expenses such as bookkeeping, advertising, accounting, laundry and cleaning services, bank fees on business accounts, legal advice, and so on

Accreditation:
a process of validation in which educational institutions are evaluated

▣ **Property taxes:** in some states, a child-care program is exempt from property taxes if the program is accredited. In most states accreditation is an additional expense to be added to your budget.

▣ **General office expenses:** utilities, telephones, paper, ink cartridges, staples, postal fees, and so on

ABC Learning Center's expeditures for the first year include the following:

EXPENSE	COST PER MONTH
Rent	$12,500
Property Tax	$40,000 (paid once yearly)
Building/Property/Bus Insurance	$2,083
Cleaning and Sanitizing	$1,000
Repairs and Maintenance	$500
Electricity	$2,000
Water/Sewer/Waste	$583
Security and Fire Alarm	$150
Personnel Salaries, Workers' Compensation and Health Insurance	$43,854

EXPENSE	COST PER MONTH
Local School Marketing	$1,667
Licenses and Staff Processing	$125
Purchases (School Supplies)	$500
Office Supplies	$667
Food Supplies	$5,000
Postage and Shipping	$42
Bank Merchant Services	$1,250
Accounting and Legal Services	$250
Accounting Licenses	$250
Equipment Lease	$146
School Bus	$1,000
Telephone and Internet	$416
Miscellaneous Expenses	$416
Total Expenses for First Year	**$932,787**

Develop the Earnings Projections

Now that you have your income and your expenses, we are ready to build your earnings projections for your first year of operations.

Cash flow:
the amount of money being transferred into and out of a business

EBITDA:
earnings before interest, tax, depreciation, and amortization

Profitability:
money that remains after all expenses are paid

Take a look at the earnings projections statement for ABC Learning Center for the first year of operations.

ASSUMPTIONS	Jan	Feb	Mar	Apr	May	Jun	Jul	Aug	Sep	Oct	Nov	Dec
Average Tuition	$962	$962	$962	$962	$962	$962	$962	$962	$962	$962	$962	$962
Enrollment	30	40	50	60	60	70	80	90	100	110	110	110
REVENUES	28,860	38,480	48,100	57,720	57,720	67,340	76,960	86,580	96,200	105,820	105,820	105,820
Expenses												
Rent	12,500	12,500	12,500	12,500	12,500	12,500	12,500	12,500	12,500	12,500	12,500	12,500
Property Tax											(40,000)	
Building / Property/Bus Insurance	2,083	2,083	2,083	2,083	2,083	2,083	2,083	2,083	2,083	2,083	2,083	2,083
Cleaning & Sanitizing	1,000	1,000	1,000	1,000	1,000	1,000	1,000	1,000	1,000	1,000	1,000	1,000
Repairs and Maintenance	500	500	500	500	500	500	500	500	500	500	500	500
Electric	2,000	2,000	2,000	2,000	2,000	2,000	2,000	2,000	2,000	2,000	2,000	2,000
Water/Sewer/Waste	583	583	583	583	583	583	583	583	583	583	583	583
Security & Fire Alarm	150	150	150	150	150	150	150	150	150	150	150	150
Personnel, health, work comp	18,316	23,088	28,860	34,632	34,632	40,404	46,176	51,948	57,720	63,492	63,492	63,492
Local School Marketing	10,000	909	909	909	909	909	909	909	909	909	909	909
Licenses & Staff Processing	125	125	125	125	125	125	125	125	125	125	125	125
Purchases (School Supplies)	500	500	500	500	500	500	500	500	500	500	500	500
Office Supplies	667	667	667	667	667	667	667	667	667	667	667	667
Food Supplies	5,000	5,000	5,000	5,000	5,000	5,000	5,000	5,000	5,000	5,000	5,000	5,000
Postage and Shipping	42	42	42	42	42	42	42	42	42	42	42	42
Bank Charges	-	-	-	-	-	-	-	-	-	-	-	-
Bank Merchant Services	1,250	1,250	1,250	1,250	1,250	1,250	1,250	1,250	1,250	1,250	1,250	1,250
Accounting/ Legal	250	250	250	250	250	250	250	250	250	250	250	250
Accounting Licenses	250	250	250	250	250	250	250	250	250	250	250	250
Equipment Lease	146	146	146	146	146	146	146	146	146	146	146	146
School Bus	1,000	1,000	1,000	1,000	1,000	1,000	1,000	1,000	1,000	1,000	1,000	1,000
Telephone & Internet	416	416	416	416	416	416	416	416	416	416	416	416
Miscellaneous Expenses	416	416	416	416	416	416	416	416	416	416	416	416
Total Expenses	57,194	52,875	58,647	64,419	64,419	70,191	75,963	81,735	87,507	93,279	133,279	93,279
EBITDA	28,334	14,395	10,547	6,699	6,699	2,851	997	4,845	8,693	12,541	27,459	12,541

When you subtract the expenses from the revenues for each month, you find the EBITDA, or earnings before interest, tax, depreciation, and amortization. You can see whether or not the center is making a profit. Profitability is whatever money remains after all expenses are paid. During the first year of operation, ABC Learning Center will operate at a loss, which is normal for some types of businesses. By July, however, ABC Learning Center is no longer losing money. In business this is called the **break-even** *point, the specific time the company is able to cover expenses.*

Year one doesn't look very good for ABC Learning Center, so the Smiths will need to paint a much brighter scenario for their prospective investors or lenders. The business plan allows them do that in the next section: the profit and loss statement projections.

Building Your Profit and Loss Statement

Banks and investors want to see a fifteen-year plan on how you intend to meet your financial objectives. Therefore, they are expecting a financial statement for the next fifteen years.

To create a fifteen-year projection, you will need to prepare your profit and loss (P and L) statement (also called an *income statement*), which shows income and expenses over a given period of time.

The income statement, or P and L, always starts with the revenues: the amount of money you collect from tuition, state support, and other funding sources. Your company might have other income as well, such as curriculum fees (for books and other materials needed to support your program) or enrollment fees (one-time or yearly fees to enroll children for the next school year).

Revenue:
how much money you make

Cost:
how much you spend

Income statement (also called a profit and loss statement or P and L statement):
a financial statement that summarizes a business's revenues, costs, and expenses incurred during a specified period

Providing food is a significant expense for the child-care facility. In some markets, there are federal food-reimbursement programs for qualifying locations.

Your accountant can set up your account registry and help you define your cost of goods sold, gross profit margins, and EBIDTA.

Cost of goods sold:

refers to the actual costs directly attributable to the production of the goods sold in a company

Gross profit:

the difference between revenue and the cost of making a product or providing a service, calculated before deducting overhead, payroll, taxes, and interest payments

EBITDA:

Earnings before interest, tax, depreciation, and amortization

ABC Learning Center's profit and loss statement for the first year looks like this:

ABC Learning Center January–December 2019

REVENUE	EXPENSES
Average Tuition $962	Rent: $12,500
School Capacity (Students) 200	Property Tax: $40,000 (paid once yearly)
Average Occupancy 55%	Building/Property/Bus Insurance: $2,083
Enrollment 110	Cleaning and Sanitizing: $1,000
	Repairs and Maintenance: $500
	Electricity: $2,000
	Water/Sewer/Waste: $583
	Security and Fire Alarm: $150
	Personnel Salaries, Health, and Workers' Comp. Ins.: $43,854
	Local School Marketing: $1,667

REVENUE	EXPENSES
	Licenses and Staff Processing: $125
	Purchases (School Supplies): $500
	Office Supplies: $667
	Food Supplies: $5,000
	Postage and Shipping: $42
	Bank Merchant Services: $1,250
	Accounting/Legal Services: $250
	Accounting Licenses: $250
	Equipment Lease: $146
	School Bus: $1,000
	Telephone and Internet: $416
	Miscellaneous Expenses: $416
Tuition Revenue $851,760	**Total Expenses for First Year: $932,787**
	EBITDA -$81,027

From the P and L, you can make fifteen-year projections. To build this, you will need to make some assumptions. Let's look at ABC Learning Center's revenue forecast.

> *ABC Learning Center assumes a tuition increase of 3 percent every year. It will operate at 55 percent capacity by the end of the first year (110 / 200 = .55). Based on their sales projections, they will reach full capacity by the end of year two.*

YEAR	BLENDED TUITION AVERAGE
1	$226,564
2	$226,564 + $6,797 = $233,361
3	$233,361 + $7,001 = $240,362
4	$240,362 + $7,211 = $247,573
5	$247,573 + $7,427 = $255,000
6	$255,000 + $7,650 = $262,650
7	$262,650 + $7,879 = $270,529
8	$270,529 + $8,116 = $278,645
9	$278,645 + $8,359 = $287,004
10	$287,004 + $8,610 = $295,614
11	$295,614 + $8,868 = $304,482
12	$304,482 + $9,134 = $313,616
13	$313,616 + $9,408 = $323,024
14	$323,024 + $9,691 = $332,715
15	$332,715 + $9,981 = $342,696

Next, you will need to project the expenses for the fifteen-year span. With these revenue and expense projections, you can develop your fifteen-year projections.

ABC Learning Center assumes an expenses increase of 3 percent every year.

ASSUMPTIONS	Y1	Y2	Y3	//	Y13	Y14	Y15
Average Tuition	$962	$989	$1,016		$1,286	$1,313	$1,340
School Capacity (Students)	200	200	200		200	200	200
Occupancy (Avg. Students)	55%	60%	63%		85%	85%	85%
Enrollment (Avg. Students)	110	120	125		170	170	170
REVENUES	**875,420**	**1,424,160**	**1,524,000**		**2,623,440**	**2,678,520**	**2,733,600**
Tuition*	875,420	1,424,160	1,524,000		2,623,440	2,678,520	2,733,600
Expenses							
Rent	150,000	150,000	174,000		210,540	210,540	210,540
Proper	40,000	41,200	42,436		57,030	58,741	60,504
Building / Property/Bus Ins	25,000	25,750	26,523		35,644	36,713	37,815
Pest C	1,000	1,030	1,061		1,426	1,469	1,513
Cleaning & Sanitizing	12,000	12,360	12,731		17,109	17,622	18,151
Repair	6,000	6,180	6,365		8,555	8,811	9,076
Electric	24,000	24,480	24,970		30,438	31,047	31,667
Water/Sewer/Waste	7,000	7,210	7,426		9,980	10,280	10,588
Security & Fire Alarm	1,800	1,854	1,910		2,566	2,643	2,723
Personnel, health, work com	525,252	783,288	838,200		1,442,892	1,473,186	1,503,480
Local School Marketing	20,000	28,483	30,480		52,469	53,570	54,672
Licenses & Staff Processi	1,500	1,530	1,561		1,902	1,940	1,979
Purchases (School Suppli	6,000	6,120	6,242		7,609	7,762	7,917
Office Supplies	8,000	8,160	8,323		10,146	10,349	10,556
Food Supplies	60,000	71,208	76,200		131,172	133,926	136,680
Postage and Shipping	500	510	520		634	647	660
Bank Charges			–		–		–
Bank Merchant Services	15,000	15,300	15,606		19,024	19,404	19,792
Accounting/ Legal	3,000	3,060	3,121		3,805	3,881	3,958
Accounting Licenses	3,000	3,060	3,121		3,805	3,881	3,958
Equipment Lease	1,750	1,785	1,821		2,219	2,264	2,309
School Bus	12,000	12,000	12,000		12,000	12,000	12,000
Telephone & Internet	5,000	5,000	5,000		5,000	5,000	5,000
Miscellaneous Expenses	5,000	5,100	5,202		6,341	6,468	6,597
	932,802	1,214,668	1,304,819		2,072,307	2,112,144	2,152,135
EBITDA	57,382	209,492	219,181		551,133	566,376	581,465

*Chart has been condensed for space. For full chart, see https://www.gryphonhouse.com/books/details/ the-basics-of-starting-a-child-care-business

BUILD YOUR KNOWLEDGE

- » How do you determine how much money you will need to start?

- » How do you identify your real estate site?

- » How do you develop your sales projection?

- » How do you calculate start-up costs?

- » How do you create a cash flow statement?

- » How to you build a profit and loss statement?

5

YOUR ORGANIZATION, STRATEGY, AND IMPLEMENTATION

_____ 〞〞 _____

Alone we can do so little; together we can do so much.

—HELEN KELLER, AUTHOR, SPEAKER,
AND POLITICAL ACTIVIST

MAIN QUESTIONS

» Who are the key employees in your organization?

» How do you intend to accomplish the goals of the business plan?

» What are your objectives for each department?

» What goals do you need to set to achieve each of your objectives?

» What steps will you take to meet each goal?

One of the keys to the success of a business is its people; therefore, give your personnel planning great and careful consideration. You can design the best program in the world, but if you are not able to recruit and retain the best executors for the vision, you will not fulfill the mission or accomplish your goals. Child-care operations include human-resources management, policies, hiring, determining staff size, management of the physical facilities, curriculum implementation, safety procedures, sales and marketing, building maintenance, and many other areas. This chapter will focus on developing the part of the business plan that describes the organization structure, management team, and staff.

THE ORGANIZATION CHART

A company's organization chart illustrates relationships among employees. Larger centers typically hire a director, an assistant director, administrative assistants, lead teachers, assistant teachers, cooks, and support personnel. Smaller centers typically have a director and the teaching staff.

ABC Learning Center Organization Chart

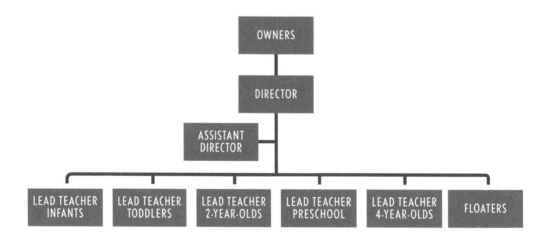

THE MANAGEMENT TEAM

Your management team comprises the key people required to run your child-care center. Lenders and investors reading your business plan are trying to understand who has the experience and skills to achieve your business goals. The basic business categories are marketing and sales, operations, and finance.

The opening team for ABC Learning Center will consist of the general manager, a director, lead teachers, and support staff. As the business grows, additional investment in instructional staff will be made gradually, as dictated by enrollment. Mr. Smith will be the general manager responsible for achieving the business goals for the sales, marketing, and finance departments. Mrs. Smith will be the onsite director responsible for overseeing customer service, human resources, operations, and compliance.

Your center director organizes the resources to achieve the business plan. Owners and directors should communicate about the expectations and goals to effectively organize the different resources and implement the business objectives. Child-care directors who have an understanding of the business side of the operation will be able to operate more efficiently and respond faster to market trends.

The secret of running a successful child-care program lies in selecting the right candidate for the director position. Directors are the heart and soul of a school. The director's job description includes a diverse range of responsibilities:

- **Human resources:** recruiting staff, training new employees, coordinating staff meetings, creating vacation times

- **Quality controls and curriculum implementation:** conducting classroom observations, assessing children, and monitoring curriculum implementation

- **Compliance and record keeping:** cooperating with licensing authorities, maintaining updated records

- **Sales and marketing:** giving tours and contacting leads

- **Customer service:** customer support and working to meet the needs of families

- **Finance:** collecting payments from families and maintaining the center budget

SETTING THE OBJECTIVES AND CREATING A STRATEGY

Practicing a skill many times leads to a certain level of mastery. I was a classical pianist and cellist for many years. I started playing the piano when I was just four years old, before I could read or write. I spent my childhood and adolescence practicing two hours of piano and two hours of cello every day, including weekends. Every year, my teacher would go over the objetives for the year and would assign musical pieces to practice. At the beginning of the year those objectives seemed overwhelming. Yet, by breaking down the objectives into simple steps, I had a clear path of what needed to be done every day to reach them.

The best way to acomplish an objective is by following simple sequential steps and regularly measuring progress. Once you have mastered those goals, you are ready for the next level. When you are compiling the information for your business plan, you must decide on your objectives for your business. What do you envision? Then think about the steps you will need to take to achieve your objectives.

Crafting the strategy and implementation plan requires a company to create a continual improvement process that will inform your business decisions and be revised as you measure your performance against your goals and expectations. Joseph Weintraub, a professor of management at Babson College and coauthor of *The Coaching Manager: Developing Top Talent in Business*, says, "We need to constantly look for opportunities to stretch ourselves in ways that may not always feel comfortable at first." The strategy and implementation summary section of the business plan identifies the milestones the business will use to grow the business and the budget for implementation during the first year of the operation. The process is simple:

- Set the objectives.

- Set up SMART goals for each objective.

- Break down each goal into small parts or action steps.

- Establish measures to check your progress.

Setting Objectives

This section will set up target results and objectives that will serve as a general guideline for your business to ensure that everyone in the company is working toward the same goals. The strategic plan contains important information on organizational objectives and includes specific goals and the activities and processes to reach those goals. Your objectives should include specific outcomes to achieve in every department: marketing, sales, finance, licensing, human resources, curriculum, accounting, customer service and retention, and operations.

Setting SMART Goals

Once you define your objectives in specific areas of the business, you are ready to break those objectives into smaller goals that will help you reach those objectives. As reported by

Duncan Haughey in the article "A Brief History of SMART Goals," business consultant George T. Doran suggested turning goals into SMART goals: specific, measurable, assignable, relevant, and time-bound. Robert Rubin, a professor at Saint Louis University, further developed the idea, changing *assignable* to *attainable*.

- ☑ **S: Specific**—What, when, where, and how?

- ☑ **M: Measurable**—What data will measure the progress?

- ☑ **A: Attainable**—What are the steps you will take to reach the goal?

- ☑ **R: Relevant**—Does this goal align with your other goals?

- ☑ **T: Time-bound**—What is your time frame for reaching this goal?

> *ABC Learning Center has created SMART goals for each of their objectives. Looking at the sales objective, the SMART goals are the following:*
>
> **Sales:** *Enroll 110 children the first year.*
>
> » **S: Specific:** *Enroll 110 children.*
>
> » **M: Measurable:** *Track new enrollments at the end of each month.*
>
> » **A: Attainable:** *Competitors are enrolling the same number of children.*
>
> » **R: Relevant:** *Relevancy ensures that the goal is important.*
>
> » **T: Time-bound:** *Sales will reach this goal within the first year of business.*

Setting Action Steps

Once you come up with your SMART goals, you are ready to start listing how you will reach them; that list becomes your action steps.

ABC Learning Center has set its objectives for the first year in business.

DEPARTMENT	OBJECTIVE	SMART GOALS
Sales	Enroll 110 children the first year.	**Specific:** Enroll 110 children. **Measurable:** Track new enrollments at the end of each month. **Attainable:** Competitors are enrolling the same number of children. **Relevant:** This ensures that the goal is important. **Time-bound:** Sales will reach this goal within the first year of business.
Marketing	Create a promotion that generates thirty prospective leads every month. Out of the thirty leads each month, ten families will enroll.	**Specific:** Enroll 110 children. **Measurable:** Track our tour-per-lead conversion. We will generate thirty leads and close ten sales. **Attainable:** Competitors are enrolling the same number of children. **Relevant:** This ensures that the goal is important. **Time-bound:** Sales will reach this goal within the first year of business.
Finance	Reach profitability and break even by July.	**Specific:** Reach the break-even point. **Measurable:** We will reach profitability by July. **Attainable:** We can achieve this by controlling our costs. **Relevant:** It is important to control costs during the start-up phase. This ensures that the goal is important. **Time-bound:** We will accomplish this objective by July.
Licensing	Obtain a state child-care license a month prior to opening.	**Specific:** Obtain a state license. **Measurable:** Track the licensing process from application to delivery. **Attainable:** Child-care rules state that inspectors have up to 45 days to complete the application. **Relevant:** To meet the goal, we must start the process two months prior to opening. **Time-bound:** Obtain the license by January.

DEPARTMENT	OBJECTIVE	SMART GOALS
Human Resources	Hire the staff required to operate the center, to meet state ratios.	**Specific:** In stages, hire the staff needed to operate the center. **Measurable:** Payroll costs will not exceed 60 percent of our revenue. **Attainable:** Benchmark reports state that payroll costs represent up to 60 percent of total monthly revenue. **Relevant:** It is important to have the necessary crew to offer great services. **Time-bound:** We will hire gradually as new students enroll in the program.
Accounting	Meet the business-plan target goals.	**Specific:** We will assign budgets to each department. **Measurable:** The difference between actual costs and the budgeted costs should not exceed 10 percent. **Attainable:** Based on projected revenues and expenses, we can achieve profitability. **Relevant:** We will reach our break-even point. **Time bound:** By July, we will reach the break-even point.

PUT IT ALL TOGETHER

For your business plan, you will create objectives and goals for each of the departments of your business. You will then compile this information into an implementation chart: a summary of your objectives, your goals for reaching each objective, your timeline, and your budget.

BUILD YOUR KNOWLEDGE

» Choose a department and decide on an objective. Then create your SMART goals for that objective.

Department:_____

Objective:_____

S: Specific	
M: Measurable	
A: Attainable	
R: Relevant	
T: Time-bound	

» Then add the goal to your implementation table.

DEPARTMENT	OBJECTIVE	GOALS/ACTION STEPS	PERSON(S) RESPONSIBLE:	TIMELINE	MEASURE	BUDGET
Sales						
Marketing						
Licensing						
Finance						
Accounting						
Human Resources						
Customer Service and Retention						
Operations						

6

APPLYING FOR FINANCING AND MEETING WITH THE BANK

_"_

If you can dream it, you can do it. All our dreams can come true, if we have the courage to pursue them.

—WALT DISNEY, IMAGINEER

MAIN QUESTIONS

» What documents will a lender require?

» What is a loan application package?

» What are the different stages of the application process?

» What is the underwriting process?

APPLYING FOR FINANCING

As an entrepreneur, I have submitted many application packages to lenders. My business plans have been accepted, challenged, improved, and rejected. What I have learned from those experiences is that allowing bankers to challenge your assumptions leads to good outcomes and improved business plans. I have also learned that some lenders focus on different types of businesses and consider the child-care businesses to be risky. Therefore, it is advisable to understand the lender's interest in the industry before applying for a commercial loan.

It is important to be prepared to assist bankers by completing loan application packages with all the supporting documents, understanding the importance of your personal finances, and preparing a detailed business plan. You will take several steps at the beginning of this new journey.

- ▣ Check your credit score.

- ▣ Gather the documentation.

- ▣ Submit the loan application package.

Check Your Credit Score

Before submitting your application, you should obtain your credit report from the major consumer credit agencies. Review the reports to identify any inaccuracies that could affect the application process. If you find any issues, get them corrected as soon as possible. Because the owner of a business is responsible for repayment of the loan, develop a personal strategy to monitor your credit score and keep it as high as possible. Do not apply for personal loans or credit cards prior to submitting your application, as these could negatively affect your credit score.

Gather the Documentation

Begin the application process by gathering all the necessary documentation to complete your application. Most lenders will require you to submit the same documents; therefore, you can use the same documentation to prepare different loan packages for different lenders. You will need the following documents and information:

Collateral:
property pledged as a guarantee of repayment of a loan, to be forfeited if the loan is not repaid

- **Loan application form:** You will have to complete one for each lending institution. On the form, you will need to provide your personal background information, including previous addresses, your social security number, and marital status.

- **Personal documents:** You will need to provide your proof of citizenship, such as a passport or driver's license.

- **Résumé:** Lenders require evidence of management or business experience, particularly for new business loans.

- **Business plan**

- **Personal credit score**

- **Business credit report**

- **Proof of funds:** You will need to provide your bank statements and proof that you have the funds for the down payment.

- **Income tax returns:** Most loan programs require applicants to submit personal income tax returns for the previous three years.

- **Financial statements:** These include balance sheets, income statements, and cash flow projections for your business.

- **Personal financial statements:** Many loan programs require owners with more than a 20 percent stake in the business to submit signed personal financial statements.

- **Collateral:** Loans involving high-risk factors for default require substantial collateral. Strong business plans and financial statements can help you avoid putting up collateral.

- **Legal documents of entity formation:** You will need to provide documentation that you have legally formed and registered your company.

- **Franchise agreements:** If you have purchased a franchise, you will need to provide all the documentation related to that purchase.

- **Commercial leases:** If you are leasing your business space or equipment, you must provide the leases for the property.

- **Business licenses:** You will need to provide your business licenses and registrations required for you to conduct business.

- **Vendor contracts:** You will need to provide copies of contracts you have with any third parties.

Submit the Application Package

When you have gathered the documentation and filled out the application forms, you will submit your application package to different lenders. Your application will give each lender authorization to pull out some pieces of information needed to make a decision, such as your credit score and the assets that you could pledge to the lender as collateral until the loan is satisfied. If you pass the credit review and the bank is comfortable with the business plan, you will be contacted for a follow-up meeting.

MEETING WITH THE BANK

The bank will conduct a preliminary review and contact you to request a meeting or a follow-up call. During this meeting, a loan officer will discuss the business plan in detail. I asked one of our bankers, Melanie DiVirgilio, to explain what she is looking for when evaluating business plans. She gave me the following list of questions.

- Will the borrower pay me back?

- Does the applicant have a track record in the industry?

- What can I accept as collateral if the business fails?

- How will the loan proceeds be used?

- What assets need to be purchased, and who are your suppliers?

- What other business debt do you have, and who are your creditors?

- Who are the members of your management team?

- Is this entrepreneur financially able to walk away from her current job to become a business owner?

- Can the operator manage cash flow?

If you pass the initial review, you might receive a commitment letter from the bank, which describes specific terms of the loan, including your interest rate. Your application will be underwritten and then approved or declined by a committee. The underwriting process will evaluate both your personal finances and your business finances; the loan request process might take months to complete. Therefore, be diligent in responding to lenders' questions, be willing to apply to different loan sources, and be patient.

If your loan is approved, you are on your way to becoming a child-care entrepreneur, an exciting journey of self-discovery, growth, and the opportunity to shape the next generation. I believe business plans help give you a vision of what is possible and allow you to create a blueprint of your strategy. The loan process will challenge you to your core and test your patience. You will find many potential obstacles during your journey. Yet, if you persevere, you are in for a great reward. Education entrepreneurs come from all sorts of backgrounds, but we all have one thing in common: We are dreamers and we want to build a better world for the generation to come.

GLOSSARY

Accreditation: a process of validation through which educational institutions are evaluated

Angel investor: someone who invests personal money in a new company

Asset: the items on a balance sheet showing the book value of property owned, such as playground equipment, fixtures, or furniture

Balance sheet: a statement of the assets, liabilities, and capital of a business at a particular point in time

Break-even point: a point in a business's lifespan when its profits are equal to the costs of running the enterprise

Business model: a framework for reaching profitability in a business, such as identifying revenue sources, customer base, products, and details of financing

Business plan: a document setting out a business's future objectives and strategies

Capital: money or assets contributed for a particular purpose, such as starting a company or investing

Capital expenditures: funds invested by a business for acquiring or maintaining fixed assets, such as land, buildings, and equipment

Cash flow: the amount of money being transferred into and out of a business, or how the cash is used from ongoing regular business activities in a given period

Cash flow statement: a financial statement that provides information on all cash a company receives from its ongoing operations and external investment sources, as well as all cash paid out for business activities and investments during a given period

Cash reserves: money a company or individual keeps on hand to meet short-term and emergency funding needs

Collateral: something of value pledged as security for the repayment of a loan

Competitor grid: a chart used to evaluate the strategies, strengths, and weaknesses of a business's competitors

Contingency: a provision for a potential adverse event, such as a lawsuit

Cost of goods sold (COGS): the actual costs directly attributable to the production of the **goods sold** in a company (compare *Expenses*)

Debt capital: capital that a business raises by taking out a loan

Debt-to-equity ratio: how much money in down payment a business owner puts into a deal compared to how much money the company still owes on the deal

Direct competitor: service provider who offers similar services to the same target market

Due diligence: research and analysis of a company or organization done in preparation for a business transaction

EBITDA: earnings before interest, tax, depreciation, and amortization

Economy of scale: a proportionate saving in costs gained by an increased level of production

Elevator pitch: a short, persuasive sales pitch

Entrepreneur: one who organizes, manages, and assumes the risks of a business or enterprise

Equity capital: capital that a business raises by selling shares of the company to investors

Expenses: general costs not directly attributable to the production of the goods sold in a company (compare *Cost of Goods Sold*)

Financial leverage: the use of borrowed money in acquiring an asset

Fiscal year: an accounting period of twelve months; does not necessarily correlate with a calendar year of January to December

Franchise: the right or license granted to an individual or group to market a company's goods or services in a particular territory

Franchise fee: initial lump sum payable upon signing a franchise contract

Gross leasable area (GLA): the size in square feet of the premises

Gross profit: the difference between revenue and the cost of making a product or providing a service; calculated before deducting overhead, payroll, taxes, and interest payments

Income statement (also called a **profit and loss statement** or **P and L statement**): a financial statement that summarizes a business's revenues, costs, and expenses incurred during a specified period, usually a fiscal quarter or year (compare *Balance sheet*). The income statement reports revenues and expenses that net to a profit or loss.

Liabilities: the money a business owes to creditors

Licensed capacity: the total number of children in care allowed in a facility

Market research: the activity of gathering information about consumers' needs and preferences

Market saturation: a situation in which a product has become overly diffused within a market

Market survey: the survey research and analysis of the market for a particular product or service, which includes the investigation into customer inclinations

Marketing differentiator: something that distinguishes a product or service from competitors to make it more attractive to a particular target market

Marketing strategy: a plan to achieve your sales goals, your marketing budget, and a general overview of the marketing mix you intend to use

Net income (also called net profit): a company's income from a specified period minus the company's cost of goods sold, expenses, and taxes from the same period

Net worth: the total assets you have minus the amount of money you owe

Operating capital: cash used for daily operations in a company

Owners' equity (also called stockholders' equity or shareholders' equity): what is left over after a company's total liabilities are deducted from its total assets

Quality-rating programs: tools used to measure child-teacher ratios, group sizes, teacher turnover, positive interactions, accreditations, activities, environments, and health practices

Positioning: market survey results showing how your target market perceives the child care in your area; this will help you create branding and marketing messages

Revenue: how much money a company generates

Secondary competition: competitors who offer higher- or lower-end versions of the same product or sell something similar to completely different audiences

Start-up: a new business venture

Target market: a particular group of consumers at whom a product or service is aimed

REFERENCES AND RECOMMENDED READING

Abel, Michael, Teri Talan, and Marina Magid. 2018. *Closing the Leadership Gap: 2018 Status Report on Early Childhood Program Leadership in the United States.* Wheeling, IL: McCormick Center for Early Childhood Leadership at National Louis University. https://mccormick-assets.floodlight.design/wp-content/uploads/2019/02/2018-LEAD-Clearinghouse-webbook_04.pdf

Abraham, Cathy. 2010. "Parents as Partners—and Customers." *Texas Child Care Quarterly* 34(1): 2–9. http://www.childcarequarterly.com/pdf/summer10_parents.pdf

Almquist, Eric, John Senior, and Nicolas Bloch. 2016. "The Elements of Value." Bain and Company. https://www.bain.com/insights/the-elements-of-value-hbr/

Andersen, Erika. 2012. "Are Leaders Born or Made?" Forbes. https://www.forbes.com/sites/erikaandersen/2012/11/21/are-leaders-born-or-made/#4b2f15748d56

Bakhshi, Hasan, et al. 2017. *The Future of Skills: Employment in 2030.* London, UK: Pearson and Nesta. https://futureskills.pearson.com/research/assets/pdfs/technical-report.pdf

Block, Peter. 1987. *The Empowered Manager: Positive Political Skills at Work.* San Francisco, CA: Jossey-Bass.

Bouffard, Suzanne. 2017. *The Most Important Year: Pre-Kindergarten and the Future of Our Children.* New York, NY: Avery.

Boyte-White, Claire. 2019. "Is Net Income the Same as Profit?" Investopedia. https://www.investopedia.com/ask/answers/122414/net-income-same-profit.asp

Carter, Margie, and Deb Curtis. 2010. *The Visionary Director: A Handbook for Dreaming, Organizing and Improvising in Your Center.* 2nd ed. St. Paul, MN: Redleaf.

ChildCare.gov. n.d. "Ratios and Group Sizes." ChildCare.gov. https://www.childcare. gov/consumer-education/ratios-and-group-sizes

Child Care Aware America. n.d. "Opening a Child Care Center: Do Your Research." Child Care Aware America. https://www.childcareaware.org/opening-child-care-center-do-your-research/

Colgate, Mark. 2018. *The Science of Service: The Proven Formula to Drive Customer Loyalty and Stand Out from the Crowd.* Vancouver, BC: Page Two Books.

Colker, Laura, and Derry Koralek. 2018. *High-Quality Early Childhood Programs: The What, Why, and How.* St. Paul, MN: Redleaf.

Connelly, Rachel, Deborah DeGraff, and Rachel Willis. 2004. *Kids at Work: The Value of Employer-Sponsored On-Site Child-Care Centers.* Kalamazoo, MI: W. E. Upjohn Institute for Employment Research. https://research.upjohn.org/cgi/viewcontent. cgi?article=1043&context=up_press

Davidson, Ellis. 2019. "The Average Time to Reach Profitability in a Start Up Company." Chron. https://smallbusiness.chron.com/average-time-reach-profitability-start-up-company-2318.html

Deane, Michael. 2019. "Top 6 Reasons New Businesses Fail." Investopedia. https://www. investopedia.com/slide-show/top-6-reasons-new-businesses-fail/#targetText=It's%20 often%20said%20that%20more,66%25%20during%20the%20first%2010.

Dempsey, Brandon. 2018. "Business Life Cycle Spectrum: Where Are You?" Forbes. https://www.forbes.com/sites/theyec/2018/01/11/business-life-cycle-spectrum-where-are-you/#4390feb3ef5e

Entrepreneur. 2019. "Location." Entrepreneur. https://www.entrepreneur.com/ encyclopedia/location

Florida Department of Children and Families. 2017. *Child Care Facility Handbook.* Florida Department of Children and Families. https://www.myflfamilies.com/service-programs/child-care/docs/handbook/Facility%20Handbook.pdf

Franchise Chatter. 2017. "Considering a Primrose Schools Franchise? Don't Overlook These 30 Important Franchise Fees." Franchise Chatter. https://www.franchisechatter. com/2017/03/16/considering-a-primrose-schools-franchise-dont-overlook-these-25-important-franchise-fees/

Gallup. 2013. *State of the Global Workplace: Employee Engagement Insights for Business Leaders Worldwide*. Washington, DC: Gallup. http://www.gallup.com/services/176735/state-global-workplace.aspx

Gallup. 2015. *State of the American Manager: Analytics and Advice for Leaders.* Washington, DC: Gallup. https://www.gallup.com/services/182216/state-american-manager-report.aspx

George Mason University Libraries. 2019. "Industry Research Resources." George Mason University Libraries. https://infoguides.gmu.edu/MKTG353/industry

Gilkey, Charlie. 2011. "The Four Key Dimensions of Business." Productive Flourishing. https://www.productiveflourishing.com/the-four-key-dimensions-of-business/

Glynn, Sarah Jane. 2012. "Families Need More Help to Care for Their Children." Child Care Fact Sheet. Center for American Progress. https://cdn.americanprogress.org/wp-content/uploads/2012/10/ChildCareFactsheet.pdf

Goddard School. n.d. "Invest in Goddard: Franchise Costs and Investment Requirements for Opening a Goddard School Franchise." Goddard School Franchise. https://www.goddardschoolfranchise.com/franchise-cost.html

Goffin, Stacie. 2013. *Early Childhood Education for a New Era: Leading for Our Profession.* New York, NY: Teachers College Press.

Goleman, Daniel. 2004. "What Makes a Leader?" Harvard Business Review. https://hbr.org/2004/01/what-makes-a-leader

Gross, Susan. 1987. "The Power of Purpose." *Exchange* 56(4): 25–29.

Hamm, Katie, and Carmel Martin. 2015. "A New Vision for Child Care in the United States: A Proposed New Tax Credit to Expand High-Quality Child Care." Center for American Progress. https://cdn.americanprogress.org/wp-content/uploads/2015/08/31111043/Hamm-Childcare-report.pdf

Haughey, Duncan. 2014. "A Brief History of SMART Goals." Project Smart. https://www.projectsmart.co.uk/brief-history-of-smart-goals.php

Helburn, Suzanne, ed. 1995. *Cost, Quality, and Child Outcomes in Child-Care Centers: Technical Report.* Denver, CO: Department of Economics, Center for Research in Economic and Social Policy, University of Colorado at Denver.

Herzfeldt-Kamprath, Rachel, and Maryam Adamu. 2014. "Why We Need a Federal Preschool Investment in 6 Charts." Center for American Progress. https://www. americanprogress.org/ issues/early-childhood/news/2014/12/09/102737/why-we-need-a-federal-preschool-investment-in-6-charts/

HiMama and The Child Care Success Company. 2019. *2019 North American Child Care Sector Benchmark Survey.* Toronto, ON: HiMama.

Holmes, Oliver Wendell, Sr. 1873. *The Autocrat of the Breakfast-Table.* Boston, MA: James R. Osgood. http://www.gutenberg.org/files/751/751-h/751-h.htm

Hunt, James M., and Joseph Weintraub. 2002. *The Coaching Manager: Developing Top Talent in Business.* Thousand Oaks, CA: Sage Publications.

Hutchinson, Kay, Kay Sohl, and Marnie Vlahos. 2004. *Developing a Child-Care Center: An Overview of the Development Process for Creating a Child-Care Center in Your Neighborhood.* N.p.: The Enterprise Foundation. https://community-wealth.org/files/downloads/tool-enterprise-child-care.pdf

Internal Revenue Service. 2019. "Business Structures." Internal Revenue Service. https://www.irs.gov/businesses/small-businesses-self-employed/business-structures

Kagan, Sharon Lynn, and Kristie Kauerz, eds. 2012. *Early Childhood Systems: Transforming Early Learning.* New York, NY: Teachers College Press.

Kenton, Will, ed. 2019. "Cash Flow Statement." Investopedia. https://www.investopedia. com/terms/c/cashflowstatement.asp

Kenton, Will, ed. 2019. "Commercial Loan Definition." Investopedia. https://www. investopedia.com/terms/c/commercial-loan.asp

Kurt, Daniel. 2019. "Are You in the World's Top 1 Percent?" Investopedia. https://www. investopedia.com/articles/personal-finance/050615/are-you-top-one-percent-world.asp

Learning Experience, The. n.d. "The EB5 Visa Program." The Learning Experience. https://www.thelearningexperience.com/eb5/abouteb5.html

Learning Experience, The. n.d. "Franchise and Real Estate—What Will You Need?" The Learning Experience. https://www.thelearningexperience.com/franchising /tle-story

Lemser, Frank. 2018. *Strategic Product Management*. Norderstedt, Germany: Books on Demand.

Lincoln, Abraham. June 16, 1858. "A House Divided." Speech at Springfield, IL. https://voicesofdemocracy.umd.edu/lincoln-a-house-divided-speech-text/

Loveless, Becton. 2019. "Is Accreditation Meaningful in Early Childhood Programs?" Education Corner. https://www.educationcorner.com/accreditation-meaningful-early-childhood-programs.html

Lowenstein, Michael. 1997. *The Customer Loyalty Pyramid*. Westport, CT: Quorum Books.

Michel, Sonya. 1999. *Children's Interests/Mothers' Rights: The Shaping of America's Child-Care Policy*. New Haven, CT: Yale University Press.

MindTools. n.d. "SMART Goals: How to Make Your Goals Achievable." MindTools. https://www.mindtools.com/pages/article/smart-goals.htm

Morgan, Harry. 2011. *Early Childhood Education: History, Theory, and Practice*. Lanham, MD: Rowman and Littlefield Publishers.

Murray, Kris. 2012. *The Ultimate Child-Care Marketing Guide: Tactics, Tools, and Strategies for Success*. St. Paul, MN: Redleaf.

National Council of Nonprofits. 2019. "Compensation for Nonprofit Employees." National Council of Nonprofits. https://www.councilofnonprofits.org/tools-resources/compensation-nonprofit-employees

National Economic Development and Law Center. 2003. *Family Child Care: Financial-Planning and Facilities-Development Manual*. Oakland, CA: National Economic Development and Law Center. http://www.buildingchildcare.org/uploads/pdfs/FCC-Manual-FINAL.pdf

National Public Radio (NPR), the Robert Wood Johnson Foundation, and Harvard T. H. Chan School of Public Health. 2016. *Child Care and Health in America*. Washington, DC; Princeton, NJ; and Cambridge, MA: NPR, the Robert Wood Johnson Foundation, and Harvard T. H. Chan School of Public Health. https://www.rwjf.org/en/library/research/2016/10/child-care-and-health-in-america.html

Office of Head Start. 2019. "Head Start Programs." Office of Head Start. https://www. acf.hhs.gov/ohs/about/head-start

Parnell, Will, and Jeanne Marie Iorio, eds. 2016. *Disrupting Early Childhood Education Research: Imagining New Possibilities.* New York, NY: Routledge.

Pelo, Ann, ed. 2008. *Rethinking Early Childhood Education.* Milwaukee, WI: Rethinking Schools.

Pianta, Robert, ed. 2012. *Handbook of Early Childhood Education*. New York, NY: The Guilford Press.

Primrose Schools. 2019. Franchise Opportunities: Path. Primrose Schools. https://franchise.primroseschools.com/path

Reno, Hilde, Janet Stutzman, and Judy Zimmerman. 2007. *Handbook for Early Childhood Administrators: Directing with a Mission.* Boston, MA: A and B Pearson.

Rohn, Jim. 2015. "Rohn: Four Straightforward Steps to Success." SUCCESS Magazine. https://www.success.com/rohn-4-straightforward-steps-to-success/

Schulman, Karen, et al. 2012. *A Count for Quality: Child Care Center Directors on Rating and Improvement Systems*. Washington, DC: National Women's Law Center and CLASP. https://www.clasp.org/sites/default/files/publications/2017/04/ ACountforQualityQRISReport.pdf

Sciarra, Dorothy June, and Anne Dorsey. 2002. *Opening and Operating a Successful Child-Care Center.* Albany, NY: Delmar.

Shane, Scott, and Chester Spell. 1998. "Factors for New-Franchise Success." MIT Sloan Management Review. https://sloanreview.mit.edu/article/factors-for-new-franchise-success/

Sinek, Simon. 2009. *Start with Why: How Great Leaders Inspire Everyone to Take Action*. New York, NY: Penguin.

Somers, Tarah, Margaret Harvey, and Sharee Major Rusnak. 2011. "Making Child-Care Centers SAFER: A Nonregulatory Approach to Improving Child-Care Center Siting." Supplement. *Public Health Reports* 126(1): 34–40.

Sosinsky, Laura Stout, Heather Lord, and Edward Zigler. 2007. "For-Profit/Nonprofit Differences in Center-Based Child Care Quality: Results from the National Institute of Child Health and Human Development Study of Early Child Care and Youth Development." *Journal of Applied Developmental Psychology* 28(5–6): 390–410.

Stanworth, John, David Purdy, and Stuart Price. 1997. "Franchise Growth and Failure in the USA and the UK: A Troubled Dreamworld Revisited." *Franchising Research: An International Journal* 2(2): 75–94.

Strock, James. 2018. *Serve to Lead: 21st-Century Leaders Manual 2.0.* 2nd ed. Phoenix, AZ: Serve to Lead Group.

Travis, Nancy, and Joe Perrault. 1981. *The Effective Day Care Director: A Discussion of the Role and Its Responsibilities.* Atlanta, GA: Save the Children Child Care Support Center.

United States Government Accountability Office (GAO). 2010. *Head Start: Undercover Testing Finds Fraud and Abuse at Selected Head Start Centers*. Testimony before the Committee on Education and Labor, House of Representatives. Washington, DC: United States GAO. https://www.gao.gov/new.items/d10733t.pdf

United States Securities and Exchange Commission. *Annual Report Pursuant to Section 13 or 15(D) of the Securities Exchange Act of 1934: Bright Horizons Family Solutions Inc.* Washington, DC: United States Securities and Exchange Commission. http://www.annualreports.com/HostedData/AnnualReportArchive/b/NYSE_BFAM_2017.pdf

US Census Bureau. 2015. "Who's Minding the Kids? Child Care Arrangements: 2011—Detailed Tables." US Census Bureau. https://www.census.gov/data/tables/2008/demo/2011-tables.html

US Department of Education. 2018. "Improving Basic Programs Operated by Local Educational Agencies (Title I, Part A)." US Department of Education. https://www2.ed.gov/programs/titleiparta/index.html

US Department of Education. 2015. *A Matter of Equity: Preschool in America.* Washington, DC: US Department of Education. https://www2.ed.gov/documents/early-learning/matter-equity-preschool-america.pdf

US Department of Health and Human Services. 2010. "Head Start Program Facts: Fiscal Year 2010." Head Start Early Childhood Learning and Knowledge Center. https://eclkc.ohs.acf.hhs.gov/about-us/article/head-start-program-facts-fiscal-year-2010

US Small Business Administration. n.d. "Build Your Business Plan." US Small Business Administration. https://www.sba.gov/tools/business-plan/1

Wood, Meredith. 2019. "What Is an SBA Loan?" Fundera. https://www.fundera.com/business-loans/sba-loans

INDEX

A

ABC Learning Center examples. *See also* case studies
 business plans and, 22–23, 24, 26, 27
 financial plans and projections and, 52–53, 54, 56–57, 58–59, 60–61, 62–63, 63–64, 64–65
 market analysis and, 32, 33, 34, 36, 37–38, 40, 41, 43
 organization, strategy, and implementation and, 69, 71, 72–73
accreditation, 58
angel investors, 54
assets, 12
average monthly tuition, 55–56

B

banks
 independent child-care providers and, 11
 meeting with, 80–81
benefits and salaries, 9
blended tuition average, 56
branding
 corporate chains and, 9
 faith-based centers and, 10
 franchises and, 12, 13
 independent child-care providers and, 5, 11
 market research and, 31, 41–43
 marketing plans and, 21
 nonprofit chains and, 10
brand-positioning, 21, 31, 41–43
break-even point, 61
Bright Horizons, 7, 11
build your knowledge
 business plans, 26, 28
 financial plan and projections, 50, 66
 market analysis, 40, 41, 44
 organization, strategy, and implementation, 73
 overview of the child-care business, 16
building your center, 48, 49–50
business licenses, 79
business models
 how to choose a business model, 7–15
 types of business models, 4–7
business plans
 appendices and, 22
 case study on, 20–21
 company description and, 23–24
 definition of, 20
 executive summary and, 21, 22–23
 failure and, 18–19
 financial plans and, 22
 financing and, 80
 independent child-care providers and, 5
 keys to success and, 21, 22–23
 location and geographical markets served and, 24–26
 main questions, 17
 market research and, 31–44
 marketing plans and, 21
 products and services and, 21
 sales projections and, 56
 starting a new small business, 19
 strategy and implementation and, 21

C

calculating expenditures, 55, 57–59
capital, 9
capital-intensive model, 9
case studies. *See also* ABC Learning Center examples
 on business plans, 20–21
 on financial plans and projections, 46
 on market analysis, 30, 40
cash flow
 cash flow statement, 55
 definition of, 59
cash reserves, 46
Census Business Builder, 25
Center for American Progress, 3
centers, purchasing an existing, 48, 50–51
child abuse, 13
child-care accident insurance, 57
child-care business, overview of
 business models and, 4–7
 demand for child-care business, 2
 and focus on the for-profit model, 15–16
 and how to choose a business model, 7–15
 main questions, 1
 market segments and, 2–4
child-care liability insurance, 57
child-care programs, 2
child-staff ratios, 5, 9
collateral, 78, 79
commercial loans, 54, 55, 78
common-area maintenance, 48
company description, 23–24
comparison grids, 25–26
competitive landscape, 31, 32–36
competitor grids, 33
contingency, 54
corporate chains
 business models and, 4, 7, 9–10
 middle-class families and, 3, 4

corporate-sponsored programs, 4
cost, defined, 61
cost of goods sold, 61, 62
credit score, 78, 79
curriculum resources
    corporate child-care centers and, 9
    faith-based centers and, 10
    franchises and, 12
    home day-care centers and, 9
    management teams and, 69
    nonprofit chains and, 10
customer service, 19, 69

D

day-care solutions, 2
demand for child-care business, 2, 30, 31
demographic profile, 51
demographic reports, 25, 26–27
direct competitors, 35
due diligence, 15

E

earnings projections, 59–61
EBITDA, 59, 61, 62
economy of scale, 6
employer-sponsored care
    business models and, 4, 5–6, 10–11
    middle-class families and, 3
    entity formation, documents of, 79
entrepreneurs, 2
executive summary, 21, 22–23
expenditures, calculating, 55, 57–59

F

failure rate
    franchises and, 14, 18–19
faith-based centers
    business models and, 4, 5, 10
    middle-class families and, 3
family caregivers/childcare, 3, 6
federal employer identification number (FEIN), 23
federal food-reimbursement programs, 61
federal Franchise Rule, 14
financial contributions
    determining your financial contribution, 53–54
    and down payment and funding sources, 47
    faith-based centers and, 10
    franchises and, 12
    and how to choose a business model, 8
    nonprofit chains and, 10
    programs serving low-income families and, 3
    programs serving middle-class families and, 4
financial management
    management teams, 69
    why do small businesses fail? 18
financial plans and projections
    about, 47

building your financial statement, 47–65
business plans and, 22
case study on, 46
and identifying the real estate site, 47–51
main questions, 45
financial statements
    and applying for financing, 79
    and deciding on funding to apply for, 54–55
    down payment and funding sources and, 47
    financial contributions and, 53–54
    and identifying the real estate site, 47–51
    profit and cost projections and, 47
    profit and loss statements and, 61–65
    projections and, 55–61
    start-up budget and, 47, 51–53
financing, applying for
    applying for financing, 77–80
    documentation for financing, 78–79
    main questions, 77
    meeting with the bank, 80–81
fiscal year, 3
food, 61
forecasted revenue and sales projections, 55, 56–57
for-profit corporations, 24
franchises
    and building your center, 49
    business models and, 4, 6–7, 12–15
    definition of, 6
    fees associated with, 13
    finding the right franchise for you, 14–15
    franchise agreements, 79
    franchise disclosure document (FDD), 14
    franchise fee, 12
    home day-care centers and, 9
    middle-class families and, 3, 4
Fundera, Inc., 54
funding. *See* financial contributions; financing, applying for
furniture, 51

G

general liability insurance, 57
general office expenses, 58
geographical markets served, 24–28
goals, 70–71, 73, 74
goods and services, 11, 12
grants, 5, 10
gross leasable area (GLA), 52
gross profit margins, 61, 62
gross receipts, 13
group care centers, 2, 4

H

Head Start, 2, 3
home day-care centers
    business models and, 4, 6, 9

high-income families and, 4
middle-class families and, 3

I

implementation, 73–75
incidental expenses, 48
income statement, 61. *See also* profit and loss statements
independent child-care providers
  business models and, 4, 5, 11
  home day-care centers and, 9
  middle-class families and, 3
in-home caregivers, 2
insurance
  start-up budget, 51
  types of, 57–58
Investopedia.com, 12, 55

K

keys to success, 21, 22–23
Kindercare Group, 7

L

land, purchasing and developing, 48, 49–50
Learning Experience, 6
lease agreement
  and applying for financing, 79
  signing a lease agreement, 48–49
licensed capacity, 34, 42
licensing, 52
limited liability companies (LLC), 24
lines of credit, 54, 56
loans
  commercial loans, 54, 55, 78
  loan applications, 78, 79, 80
  SBA loans, 54–55
location and geographical markets served
  business plans and, 24–28
  why do small businesses fail? 18–19
low-income parents, 2, 3

M

main questions
  financial plan and projections, 45
  financing and meeting with the bank, 77
  market analysis, 29
  organization, strategy, and implementation, 67
  overview of the child-care business, 1
management
  home day-care centers and, 9
  management teams, 68–69
  why do small businesses fail? 18
market analysis
  about, 30–31
  case study on, 30, 40
  conducting market research, 31–44
  main questions, 29

market differentiators, 35, 42
market research
  brand-positioning and, 31, 41–43
  competitive landscape and, 31, 32–36
  definition of, 30, 31
  market survey and, 31, 38–40
  product description and, 31, 32
  SWOT analysis and, 31, 36–38
market saturation, 34, 35
market survey
  conducting a market survey, 38–40
  definition of, 39
  market research and, 31
marketing
  business plans and, 21
  faith-based centers and, 10
  franchises and, 12
  home day-care centers and, 9
  independent child-care providers and, 11
  management teams and, 69
  marketing strategy, 42
  nonprofit chains and, 10
  start-up budget and, 51
  why do small businesses fail? 18
middle-class parents, 2, 3–4
mission statement, 22–23

N

National Council of Nonprofits, 10
net worth, 12
nonprofit chains
  business models and, 4, 5, 10
  company description and, 24
not-for-profit settings, 2
nursery care, 4

O

objectives, setting, 69–70
operations
  home day-care centers and, 9
  operational plan, 21
  operations budget, 52
organization, strategy, and implementation
  about, 68
  main questions, 67
  management team and, 68–69
  organization chart and, 68
  put it all together and, 73–75
  setting the objectives and creating a strategy and, 69–73
overview of the child-care business. *See* child-care business, overview of
owner-operator model, 50

P

P and L statements. *See* profit and loss statements
partners, 7, 21

payroll, 58

peer support network

    faith-based centers and, 10

    franchises and, 12

    home day-care centers and, 9

    nonprofit chains and, 10

playgrounds, 51

positioning, defined, 42. *See also* brand-positioning

preoperating expenses, 52

Primrose, 6

product description, 31, 32

products and services, 11, 12, 21

professional experience, 8

professional services, 58

professional-development opportunities, 9, 12

profit and cost projections, 47

profit and loss statements

    building your financial statement and, 61–65

    definition of, 61

    financial plans and, 22

profitability, 59, 61

projections, developing

    average monthly tuition and, 55–56

    cash flow statement and, 55

    earnings projections and, 59–61

    expenditures and, 55, 57–59

    forecasted revenue and sales projections and, 55, 56–57

property insurance, 58

property taxes, 58

public schools, preschools in, 3, 4

purchasing an existing center, 48, 50–51

purchasing land and developing your project, 48, 49–50

R

real estate

    building your center and, 48, 49–50

    existing centers and, 48, 50–51

    financial statements and, 47–51

    franchises and, 12

    and identifying the site, 47–48

    independent child-care providers and, 11

    lease agreements and, 48–49

    location and geographical markets served and, 25

    repurposing real estate, 48, 49

    why do small businesses fail? 18–19

repurposing real estate, 48, 49

revenue, 61

risk tolerance, 8

S

salaries and benefits, 9

secondary competitors, 35

security deposits, 52

service positioning, 31, 41–43. *See also* brand-positioning

SMART goals, 70–71, 73, 74

staff-child ratios, 5, 9

starting a new business, 19

start-up

    definition of, 19

    start-up budget, 47, 51–53

    start-up cost expenses, 22

strategy and implementation, 21, 70–71

SWOT analysis

    brand-positioning and, 41

    conducting, 36–38

    market research and, 31

    marketing plans and, 21

T

target market, 33, 42

taxes

    company description and, 24

    faith-based centers and, 10

    loan applications and, 79

    location and geographical markets served and, 25

    nonprofit chains and, 10

    property taxes, 58

tenant improvement allowance, 49

toys and materials, 51

trade area, 25

triple net lease, 49

tuition/tuition rate

    average monthly tuition, 55–56

    faith-based centers and, 10

    home day-care centers and, 9

    nonprofit chains and, 10

turnover rate, 5, 16

U

upper-class parents, 2, 4

US Census Bureau, 25

US Department of Education, 3

US Department of Health and Human Services Administration, 3

US Small Business Association

    business locations and, 25

    business plans and, 20

    business structure and, 23

    SBA loans, 54–55

    on small businesses, 18

V

vendor contracts, 79

W

workers' compensation insurance, 58

Z

zoning laws, 25